Exploring Possibilities!

Journeying Through Career-Related Learning in Grades 4–6

A Teaching Toolkit

Lorraine Godden, Nicki Moore, Heather Nesbitt & Stefan Merchant

Exploring Possibilities! Journeying Through Career-Related Learning in Grades 4–6 A Teaching Toolkit © Lorraine Godden, Nicki Moore, Heather Nesbitt and Stefan Merchant (2024)

Published by:
CERIC
Foundation House
Suite 300, 2 St. Clair Avenue East
Toronto, ON
M4T 2T5

Website: www.ceric.ca
Email: admin@ceric.ca

ISBN
Print book: 978-1-988066-85-1
Ebook: 978-1-988066-87-5
ePDF: 978-1-988066-86-8

Design and layout: Lindsay Maclachlan, White Walnut Design

Cover illustration courtesy of iStock Photo

Table of Contents

Introducing the Authors

Dr. Lorraine Godden

Lorraine Godden PhD is a senior partner of Ironwood Consulting and a Faculty Lead in Yorkville University's Educational Master's program. Lorraine's research is rooted in understanding how educators interpret policy and curriculum to make sense of career development and employability, work-integrated learning, adult education, school-to-work transition, and other educational multidisciplinary and public policies. Her research has been published in national and international journals and conferences, and she has successfully completed many collaborative, empirical, and community-based research projects that have informed theory, policy, and practice-based initiatives. Lorraine is a qualified teacher, and has taught on Bachelor of Education, Master of Education, and a variety of career development programs for many years. Lorraine serves on the Board of Directors of the Asia Pacific Career Development Association, is an Associate at the International Centre for Guidance Studies at the University of Derby and a Fellow of the Higher Education Academy.

Nicki Moore

Nicki Moore is a Senior Lecturer in Career Development at the International Centre for Guidance Studies at the University of Derby in the UK where she leads the Centre's programme of continuing professional development. Nicki qualified as a Careers Adviser in 1996 and worked in practice for 12 years specialising in working with young people and a range of disadvantaged groups including young people with learning difficulties and disabilities, the traveller community, and those from minority ethnic backgrounds. She went on to specialise in the careers education curriculum and has researched and written widely about school and college-based careers education and personal guidance. Nicki was an Associate at International Centre for Guidance Studies at the University of Derby before joining the Centre as a full-time member of staff in July 2009. Nicki is a Fellow of the UK's Career Development Institute, a Fellow of the National Institute for Careers Education and Counselling and a Senior Fellow of the Higher Education Academy.

Dr. Heather Nesbitt

Heather Nesbitt PhD is an educator, researcher, and mother. She is an Adjunct Assistant Professor in the Faculty of Education at Queen's University and an Instructor in the School of Education at Trent University, where she works with graduate students and pre-service teachers. Heather is an Ontario qualified Primary/Junior teacher with over fifteen years of experience at both the early primary and post-secondary levels. As a researcher and educator, she is passionate about nurturing student thriving, well-being, and play, and her work contributes to the understanding of what it means to thrive across the lifespan. Heather's doctoral research offered insight into some of the critical success conditions necessary for student thriving within the kindergarten context. Comparably, she has published on and engaged in collaborative work exploring student well-being and thriving among professional and graduate students within institutions of higher education. Heather is an advocate for the child's right to play and serves on the board of directors for the International Play Association (IPA) Canada. Moreover, Heather is a mother to an active and inquisitive six-year-old who keeps her busy and playing.

Dr. Stefan Merchant

Stefan Merchant PhD is the founder of SM Research and an assistant adjunct professor at Queen's University. As an assessment researcher, Stefan specializes in the assessment of foundational skills such as responsibility, collaboration, and communication. Stefan's research has led to numerous publications including journal articles, book chapters, technical reports, and conference presentations. Stefan's extensive professional experience in the field of education as a teacher and school-based administrator means that he strives to ensure his work is practical, useful, and will result in positive changes in schools. He is currently on the executive of the Canadian Educational Research Association.

Acknowledgments

We would like to acknowledge a number of very special people who have contributed to the creation of this teaching toolkit. First, our thanks to the many educators, students, parents, business and industry partners, and teacher candidate participants. We thank you sincerely for sharing your rich insights and precious time with us. Second, we thank all the individuals and organizations from the pan-Canadian career development field and beyond who so enthusiastically helped us recruit folks to participate and offered motivating words and support throughout this project.

We would be amiss if we also did not thank the many educators across Canada and the world who consistently and enthusiastically work every day to make their students' lives better. The career-related learning you undertake is so important, and we hope we have provided some validation for your work through this toolkit. We applaud each and every one of you!

We are indebted to CERIC for making this project possible through generous funding, ongoing support, and much appreciated flexibility as we navigated the challenges of undertaking a research project during a worldwide pandemic. We are particularly thankful for the special efforts and ongoing enthusiasm of Dr. Alexandra Manoliu, Riz Ibrahim, Sharon Ferriss, and Norman Valdez on this project. A heartfelt "thank you" to you all!

Research Team

Principal Investigators

Dr. Lorraine Godden
Ironwood Consulting

Nicki Moore
International Centre for Guidance Studies (iCeGS)
University of Derby

Dr. Heather Nesbitt
Faculty of Education
Queen's University

Dr. Stefan Merchant
Faculty of Education
Queen's University

Funders

CERIC
Foundation House
2 St. Clair Avenue East
Suite 300
Toronto, ON
M4T 2T5

Preface

This teaching toolkit responds to an important question: Why should elementary education be concerned with career? This is a good question to ask as we typically think of elementary education as being about teaching and learning for the development of children rather than developing children for a career.

We realize that there are justifiable concerns about undertaking career-related learning in elementary education, as terms such as *career development* and *career education* are often linked with *careers guidance* and the making of choices during secondary education about post-secondary destinations and work. Some educators and parents may worry that career-related learning in elementary schools might be leading children towards particular career pathways or jobs when instead children should be exploring all opportunities that learning and life has to offer. We agree that we should not be expecting elementary age children to be committing to which jobs they see themselves applying for at this stage of their lives.

However, in responding to these concerns, it is helpful to think a little more about *career* and what career is, to see beyond *jobs* and realize the breadth and depth of what *career* consists of. Career is about *life*, *learning*, and *work*. Therefore, career concerns everyone, is for everyone, and encompasses the learning we undertake from birth throughout life. Through our work for this toolkit, we have seen that, in fact, many educators understand and align with this definition of career.

> [Career is...] *"A life-long journey one takes filled with of different education and work experiences; using and identifying different knowledge, skills and personal qualities and characteristics that make a positive contribution to the work one is doing and the community one is living in."* (Grade 6 teacher participant)

When viewed through this lens, it becomes easier to see why we should be thinking about career in elementary schools, especially when we acknowledge that young children of elementary school age are developing skills and experiences that build their capacity for successful learning and positive, harmonious career and life outcomes. Nevertheless, many elementary school teachers may not be fully aware of how their day-to-day teaching activities connects to their important role in developing these critical career-related skills and attributes with their students. Consequently, this teaching toolkit helps to shine a light on the value and many ways of undertaking career-related learning in elementary schools.

> *"Ignoring the process of career development occurring in childhood is similar to a gardener disregarding the quality of the soil in which a garden will be planted."* (Niles & Harris Bowlsbey, 2017, p. 276)

In this teaching toolkit, we take you on a journey to explore what effective career-related learning might look like in your classroom, school, or teaching context. Throughout this journey, we hope to dispel any fear you may have about introducing career to elementary school learners and, instead, inspire you to engage in this important work. We also hope to highlight the valuable career-related learning contributions already being made by educators across Canada and beyond to help you consolidate your teaching and work with students through the lens of career-related learning.

In this toolkit, we use the term *career-related learning* to encompass the activities undertaken in elementary schools that provide students with a diverse range of experiences and opportunities to learn about themselves, increasing the focus on the learning and skills they will need to help them through education and beyond, and deepening your understanding of how this learning will benefit your students to lead harmonious lives achieving lifelong fulfillment and well-being.

Why this teaching toolkit?

This teaching toolkit is firmly rooted in the authors' shared beliefs in public education as a public good and in the instrumental role of elementary education in helping children "discover their passions and aspirations, develop their potential, and find their place in society" (Schleicher, 2018, p. vii). This toolkit is also underpinned by published literature and data we have collected from educators who were asked to shed light on how they approach the development of foundational skills in their practice and parents, students, and industry partners who were asked to share their perceptions of and what they know about career-related learning in Canadian elementary schools.

> *"Education systems play a unique and critical role in ensuring that every student has the supports they need to transition to pursue their preferred futures."*
> (Council for Ministers of Education Canada, 2017, p. 5)

In developing this toolkit, we aim to help all educators understand and showcase the various ways that their teaching practices introduce and develop foundational career-related skills, such as healthy habits of mind and being, social and emotional skills, self-confidence, and self-efficacy. Little is currently known about teacher practices in this field and the necessity of addressing this knowledge gap has been identified in several research studies (e.g., Hartung et al., 2005; Watson & McMahon, 2005). We understand from Cahill and Furey's (2017) work that young children are interested in the chores and tasks of the work undertaken by their family members, and children can express hopes and aspirations (Chambers et al., 2018).

Our hope is that this teaching toolkit will inspire and stimulate educators to journey with us as we explore and unpack career-related teaching and learning for children in grades 4–6.

Who is this teaching toolkit for?

This teaching toolkit is for anyone who is concerned with helping young children learn and develop the various skills they need to successfully navigate their learning through school and beyond.

We deliberately use the term *educators* in this toolkit to encompass all adults who work with and support children in the grade 4–6 range (typically ages 9–12). Such roles may include teachers, pre-service teachers, educational assistants, guidance counsellors, school administrators, pre-service teachers, and community partners (e.g., BGC Canada). We use the term *students* and *learners* to primarily focus on young people who are attending Canadian schools and are in grades 4–6. However, the contents of this toolkit can easily be adapted for undertaking career-related learning with many young children. We use the term *parents* as an all-encompassing term that includes all adults who play a caring role for young children, including guardians, carers, and other family members. We use the term *business and industry partners* to include for example, local employers, local charities, work-force development boards, chambers of commerce, and business education councils who may forge partnerships or have interests in the well-being of young students in their locale. Finally, this toolkit may also be of interest to folks who develop curriculum for schools, including Ministry of Education staff and policymakers.

If you are interested in helping ensure young children are on a pathway to leading healthy, informed, and fulfilling lives, then this teaching toolkit is for you.

How to interact with this teaching toolkit?

We begin with a preface, which you are currently reading, and chapter one, the introduction to our study. These sections are then followed by six further chapters, all of which can be read in order of appearance or individually. We conclude the toolkit by asking *where next in this journey?* We have intentionally structured the teaching toolkit in this way to provide flexibility for you to use the toolkit and interact with and apply elements of the toolkit to your practice in the best way for your specific context.

We have used the metaphor of *journey* throughout this toolkit. This metaphor speaks to both the journey we take with young people as they move through life and educational systems and institutions, engaging in both formal and informal learning as they move towards adulthood and increased independence, and the journey we take as educators through engaging in career-related learning with our students.

As you journey through each section of the teaching toolkit, you will notice there are common features, with the topic chapters sharing the following structure:

Exploring the possibilities	**What is this chapter about?**
	Why should I be reading this chapter?
Planning and packing for the journey	**What do I need to be thinking about?**
	• What is this topic about?
	• In the broader context
	• In my classroom
	• What does the research say?
	• Academic sources
	• Connections to our research
Experiencing the journey	**How does this chapter come to life in my classroom?**
	• Implications for practice
	• Opportunities
	• The scope of this topic
	• Activities
Evaluating the journey	**How do I know this is worthwhile?**
Journey reflections	**Key takeaways**

A note on resources, links, and URLs

We have included a range of resources, links, and URLs for you to consider as you plan for and undertake career-related learning in your context. We believe these resources provide a broad overview of the many possible sources available, and we also believe it important to acknowledge to valuable work that is being done to support effective career-related learning in elementary schools.

We are not suggesting you must use all the resources contained in this toolkit. Rather, we provide a range of sources that offer diverse perspectives and a variety of approaches. This information can be helpful as you think through what might work effectively in your specific context. We encourage you to see these resources as a starting point, to add to those you already use, building a library that you can tap into as needed.

Please note that at time of publication, all resources were current, but websites are fluid and changing. Despite this, most resources should still be accessible through an appropriate internet browser search.

Our hopes for this toolkit

We hope this toolkit will help you to see the importance of engaging in a variety of career-related activities with young students that introduce and develop foundational concepts and skills, such as healthy habits, social and emotional skills development, helping children to build their self-confidence, empathy, collaboration skills, and ways to live with harmony and balance. Such concepts and skills are crucial for successful career development in all life-stages, but they are not usually undertaken through a *career development* lens by grade 4–6 teachers. It is our hope that journeying through this toolkit will help you to affirm your current practices and yearn to learn more. You do not have to learn everything there is to know about career-related learning in elementary schools in one go, and you can move through the sections of the toolkit of most interest to you. The most important thing is to understand the value of and embrace the opportunity to undertake career-related learning in elementary schools.

Let's begin our journey...

Chapter 1
Introduction

Across Canada, provinces and territories have implemented a variety of educational strategies, initiatives, policies, and programs to help young people achieve productive and fulfilling lives, including:

- Social studies curricula (e.g., Saskatchewan, Northwest Territories, Nunavut, and Prince Edward)
- Career education/development curriculum (e.g., British Columbia, Yukon, Manitoba, Newfoundland and Labrador, and Ontario)
- Social and emotional learning initiatives (e.g., Alberta)
- Personal wellness and health (e.g., Alberta, New Brunswick, and Nova Scotia)
- Core competencies (all jurisdictions)

Ministries, school boards, and schools have a range of frameworks and policies that are attentive to the roles of educators in helping students develop foundational skills, varied interests and attributes, and a range of ways that young children can be encouraged to think about their next steps in learning. Interestingly, all these strategies, initiatives, policies, and programs contribute to and shape what we describe as career-related learning in elementary schools.

> *"Career related learning can be seen as a mechanism that informs and supports a child to develop their sense of self and a way of developing a positive and meaningful identity."* (Kashefpakdel et al., 2018a, p. 2)

However, we know that several challenges impact the successful implementation of such policies, which in turn may affect young people as they try to successfully navigate through school and subsequent steps and life stages (Gallagher-Mackay, 2019). For instance, many elementary schools have limited resources beyond the classroom teacher to support students' career and life planning (e.g., Gallagher-Mackay, 2019; Kashefpakdel et al., 2018b). For example, in Ontario, only 25% of elementary schools have access to a guidance counsellor (People for Education, 2016) even though more than 80% of schools report that guidance counsellors play a primary role in supporting students' mental health, academic achievement, transitions, and development and refinement of individual pathways. Therefore, the undertaking of any career-related learning often falls to the classroom teacher, who may or may not be fully aware of this responsibility but are, in-fact, often responding to this duty through their day-to-day practice.

One of the purposes of this teaching toolkit was to respond to some of these challenges through a multi-year research project undertaken by the toolkit authors that investigated:

a. What are current education policies and curriculum that facilitate career-related learning in Canadian elementary public schools?
b. How are these policies and curriculum manifested into teaching practices to facilitate career-related learning? and
c. What is the grade 4–6 students' understandings of, and experiences with, career-related learning?

An overarching goal of the research project was to contribute to CERIC's two strategic mandates by undertaking a thorough investigation and analysis of the current landscape of how career-related foundational skills are being developed through grades 4–6 in elementary schools across Canada, advancing CERIC's position as a credible and valuable source of expertise within this field.

CERIC's Two Strategic mandates

Promoting career development as a priority for the public good

Building career development knowledge, mindsets, and competencies

Through our work, the project team was committed to supporting and advocating for the sustained effort of improving economic and social well-being of both our research participants and wider populations through learning, personal, and career development services, programs, and initiatives.

Aims of this teaching toolkit

The overarching aims of this teaching toolkit are to:

1. Explore understandings of career and career-related learning as they relate to teaching in grades 4–6
2. Collate knowledge of different practices in delivering effective career-related learning
3. Increase understanding of the barriers and enablers (conditions and strategies) to worthwhile practices in career-related learning
4. Document innovative and creative practices and example activities including the use of digital technology to deliver career-related learning
5. Illustrate ways educators can work with their local and broader communities to support their effectiveness in the delivery of career-related learning
6. Provide examples of ways to evaluate teaching of career-related learning for grades 4–6

Underpinning research and evidence

As a research team, our interest in young people's career development is well-established and we saw this project as a perfect opportunity to develop a deeper and more global understanding of this important area. Currently, research into the efficacy of career-related learning and career development in the early years and elementary schools is limited. This pan-Canadian project contributes new perspectives and insights into what works, promising practices, and recommendations for the further development of career-related learning programming within Canada and beyond.

Summary of key findings from previous research

This teaching toolkit is underpinned by a broad body of previously undertaken scholarly work in addition to the research completed by the authors of this toolkit. Investigating the role of career-related learning and career development in elementary schools has aimed to facilitate the development of appropriate theory, research, and practice of career development for young children (e.g., Hartung et al., 2008; Waston & McMahon, 2008).

Some of the prior research has explored:

- The importance of the early experiences of children and the impact of these experiences on future career planning (e.g., Magnuson, 2000)
- Career adaptability (e.g., Hartung et al., 2008)
- How young children envisage their futures (e.g., Chambers et al., 2018)
- The role of parents as a potential influencer in the career development of young children (e.g., Chavaudra et al., 2014)
- The role of educators as the earliest facilitators of career development (e.g., Kashefpakdel et al., 2018a, 2019).

Career development work with young children has been examined by some Canadian researchers, most notably in the Canadian context through the work of Cahill and Furey (2017) who sought to identify gaps in developmental theory and practice for career development for pre-school to grade 3 students, their parents, educators, and the wider community.

Despite the work that has been completed to date, key barriers to providing effective career education in schools remain, including:

- Time
- Prioritization
- Buy-in from school leaders
- Division of labour throughout schools
- Embedding career-related learning throughout the curriculum
- Working effectively with parents and carers
- Geography challenges
- Teachers' knowledge
- Networks and brokerage
- The tension between expanding horizons and whittling down options (Millard et al., 2019)

Amidst this milieu, there is a growing body of research examining what helps young children thrive in their early years at school (e.g., through their development of self-regulation, self-efficacy, confidence). This teaching toolkit and the research that it is informed by brings together what is known about helping young children to thrive and how this knowledge intersects with and underpin the foundations of effective career-related learning. By seeing the immense potential benefits that come from undertaking effective career-related learning in elementary schools, we believe that many of the identified challenges can be mitigated and even overcome.

Our research study of career-related learning in grades 4–6

In our project, we used a mixed method, multi-phase approach to respond to the research questions, ensuring that we gathered data from educators, parents, and grade 4–6 students in public school settings across Canada and individuals within the wider business and industry communities. Our main ways of collecting data were:

Table 1.
Data collection methods

Literature Review	Environmental scan (e.g., business and industry connections)
Environmental scan (e.g., curriculum documents, school-based career-related policies)	Surveys: Educators, Trainee teachers, Parents & carers, Students, Industry partners

In total, we conducted an extensive literature review that explored career-related learning for grades 4–6, an environmental scan of all career-related learning curriculum documents across the ten provinces and three territories of Canada, and an environmental scan of websites of business and industry councils that have partnerships and/or relationships with elementary schools located in Canada. In addition, we surveyed 319 parents, educators, teacher candidates, students, and business and industry partners, with surveys conducted in English and French. Survey participants were asked to share their understandings of career, rank a variety of skills they believed were essential to support students' life, learning, and work skills development. In addition, participants were asked to define career, and consider the importance of a range of skills they would typically develop with their students, when students should be introduced to career-related learning, share information about the type of career-related activities they typically engage in, and the types of resources they have available to them. More detail of what we investigated is included in Table 2.

Table 2.

Overview of the career-related topics investigated in our study

Data collection strategy	What we investigated
Literature Review	The review explored the scholarly literature related to career development terminology, appropriate career development frameworks and theoretical understandings, and empirical work that examined the ways teachers introduce and develop foundational career skills (e.g., healthy habits of mind and being, social and emotional skills, selfconfidence, self-efficacy).
Environmental Scan – Curriculum	We conducted a pan-Canadian scan of key curriculum and policy documents (Grades 4, 5, and 6). Publicly available documents were collected from provincial and territorial government websites (available as of July 2020). Where available, three types documents were collected: (a) career development curriculum and/or policy documents; (b) subject area curriculum documents; and (c) report cards. Career development curriculum and/or policy documents were closely reviewed and analyzed. Subject area curriculum documents and report cards were scanned for the inclusion of career-related content. In addition, we conducted a targeted scan for the term "career" in all collected subject area documents.
Environmental Scan – Industry Partnerships	The analysis included publicly available federal, provincial, and territorial business and industry community websites allowing us to establish where and how the wider business and industry community were providing services, programming, training, resources, or partnerships to and with elementary schools across Canada.
Survey	We examined how teachers in grades 4–6 develop critical transferrable skills, such as communication, teamwork, and adaptability, and career-related learning. We also asked teachers to share their thoughts on career and career-related learning in elementary schools. We also sought to learn more about what educators and people who work with children in grades 4–6 (approximate age 8–12) think about such skills, and in particular which skills they feel that young children should be developing that will support them through their schooling and eventually into work. We surveyed teacher candidates, parents, industry partners, and students.

Key findings from our study

Our study findings are dispersed throughout this toolkit by topic area. In this introductory chapter, we share the findings of an important question asked to respondents about when career-related learning in schools should begin. We share insights from educators, students, and parents in response to this question.

When do educators feel that should career-related learning should begin?

The educator respondents to our survey all agreed that career-related learning should begin in elementary school. When asked *"At what grade level should students begin developing an understanding about careers and the world of work?"* the most common response was kindergarten or grade 1 and the highest age range selected by any respondent was *"grades 7 to 9"* (selected by one respondent). No respondent selected the response option that *"Careers and the world of work should not be part of K–12 schooling."* The responses to this item were consistent with those of a later item that asked at what age is it appropriate for students to start exploring possible career paths. The most common response to this item was *"Younger than 6,"* and the oldest response (selected by one person) was the 13 to 15 age range. Clearly, elementary educators feel it is appropriate for young children to begin learning about careers and the world of work.

When do pre-service teachers feel that should career-related learning should begin?

Among the pre-service teachers who responded to this item, there was little consensus about when career education should begin. When asked *"At what grade level should students begin developing an understanding about careers and the world of work?"* the most common responses were *"grades 4 to 6"* and *"grades 7 to 9"* (each was selected by 31% of respondents), followed by *"grades 2 or 3"* and *"kindergarten or grade 1"* (each was selected by 15% of respondents). Another item later in the survey asked at what age is it appropriate for students to start exploring possible career paths. Pre-service teachers generally felt that early to mid-adolescence was the appropriate time for students to begin learning about careers and the world of work. The most common response to this item was the 13 to 15 age range (33% of respondents) followed by the 10 to 12 age range (27% of respondents). Compared to practicing educators, pre-service teachers responded that career education should begin later in a child's life. These findings might indicate that because pre-service teachers are commonly in the early stages of their own careers, they are still developing their deeper understanding of career-related learning in educational contexts.

When do students feel that should career-related learning should begin?

The respondents to the student survey showed a range of responses (with no clear favourite) as to when career related learning should begin it school with eight-years-old being the youngest response option selected and sixteen or older being the oldest. Compared to the educators, students thought that career education should begin later in the schooling process. The difference in the educator and student responses may reflect their differing conceptions of what constitutes "career."

While there was disagreement about when career education should begin, there was general agreement that learning about careers is interesting, with 75% of respondents labeling learning about careers as "interesting" or "super interesting."" This finding is consistent with the educator data that showed that teachers think students like learning about careers and jobs.

All respondents to the student survey were able to cite an example of a classroom activity that could be described as career-related (e.g., a field trip, guest speaker, or researching a specific career). One of the respondents described a field trip to the parliament buildings in Ottawa as career-related because they learned about the jobs that

members of parliament do. This may not fall under everyone's definition of career-related, but the overall finding is that most students remember career-related activities from their classrooms.

When do parents feel that should career-related learning should begin?

When asked general questions about their support for career education in elementary school, parents were generally positive. The percentage of respondents who selected either "strongly agree" or "somewhat agree" (there was no "agree" option) is reported for each item in Table 3. The general theme is that parents see value in career education and think it should be a topic of discussion and learning for their child(ren). It was interesting to note that 71% of parents said their child(ren) asks questions about jobs and careers compared to 100% of educators.

Table 3.
Percentage of parents who agreed with statements relating to career education.

Statement	Percentage who agreed
It is appropriate for Grade 5 students to be thinking about their future career path	70%
Elementary teachers play a vital role in developing career related skills	82%
Elementary schooling has a big influence on students' career choices	62%
Career education should be explicitly included somewhere in the curriculum in Grades 4 to 6.	65%
My child(ren) ask(s) about jobs, careers, and work	71%
I discuss careers, jobs, and the world of work with my child(ren)	90%

About one third (31%) of parent respondents said parents should bear the primary responsibility in guiding students towards future careers. However, almost an equal number (27%) thought this responsibility should fall primarily on teachers. A small number of respondents (4%) to this item indicated that career education is not appropriate for students in grades 4 to 6.

From the remaining respondents who were asked *"At what grade level should students begin developing an understanding about careers and the world of work?"* about 24% of respondents said that grades 4 to 6 was the correct time. The most popular option was grades 7 to 9, which was selected by 33% of respondents. Only 6% of respondents thought that this understanding should be developed in high school (grades 10 to 12), with the remaining respondents (37%) thinking it should happen in grade 3 or earlier (including 12% who thought it should happen in pre-school).

Interestingly, when respondents answered a similar question on the survey about "What age should children start exploring career paths?" the most popular response was 10 to 12 years old (selected by 32% of respondents) followed by 13 to 15 years old (26% of respondents).

About 26% of respondents selected 8 years old or less. In short, there is a consistent picture that parents see late childhood or early adolescence as the appropriate time to begin career education and exploration.

What to expect from this toolkit

Throughout this toolkit, you will see that we have underpinned the topics with findings from empirical studies and, most importantly, varied quotations and data from the students, parents, teachers, teacher candidates, and business and industry partners who have willingly shared their thoughts with us.

Chapter 2
Talking About Career

Exploring the possibilities: What is this chapter about?

In this chapter, we explore what is means to talk about careers, why it is important, and how educators and other career influencers can work towards a common understanding of career-related vocabulary, terminology, and concepts to improve career conversations.

Research highlights the need for young students to build career literacy. In fact, career-related vocabulary and terminology are the building blocks to effective career research and conversations (Moore & Hooley, 2012). However, differences in the use and understanding of career-related vocabulary, as well as varied conceptions of career development and career-related learning, can complicate conversations among students and adults both within and outside the classroom (Moore & Hooley, 2012).

Many adults, such as parents, teachers, neighbours, media personalities, and extended family members, are often referred to as *career influencers* (Ho, 2019) and can influence a child's thinking about their career. Even though the term "career" is used regularly within conversations among students and career influencers, the word itself is complex to define.

Why should I be reading this chapter?

There are concerns that elementary school is too early to begin thinking and talking about career. This toolkit responds to that notion and provides evidence on why it is important that we start positive and productive career-related conversations with young children. As we consider these conversations, thinking about the language that we use to talk about career-related issues is crucial. Elementary school is a time when young people are exploring their environment and the roles of the people around them. We would be doing young people a disservice if we did not equip them with the tools and, in this case, the vocabulary to enter conversations, and to equip them to understand and interpret the world around them. Career-related vocabulary is helpful in this instance, as you will see through reading this chapter. Importantly, this chapter will help you to think about the common career-related words and how to ensure that your students learn them in a way that will enhance their understanding.

This isn't the end of the story however! Research has shown that adults also have some very diverse understandings of common career-related words. Let's start with the word *Career* itself. If you were to ask the educators in your school to define the word, how many definitions would you get? It might be worth testing that idea! So, this chapter also helps you to think about how you might work with your colleagues to come to some common understanding and uses of career-related terminology.

Planning and packing for the journey: What do I need to be thinking about?

Career: A complex term

Let's begin by exploring the word career. *Career* can be both a noun (to have a career) or a verb (to career through a succession of opportunities). To some, the concept of career is limited to the paid work that adults undertake to earn money, hence the term *career* gets substituted by the term *employment*. To others, career is a sequence of events through the totality of one's life including learning, paid work, unpaid work, and other events that influence our life's pathway.

Moore and Hooley's (2012) research provided evidence of this range of definitions and understandings by asking young people aged 11 to 19 years to define the word *career*. While all research participants could offer an explanation, there were many variations among the definitions. Interestingly, the definitions became more sophisticated as the young participants increased in age. However, even then there were some differences. What was notable was how some young people explained that they did not like the word *career* and only used it when engaging with teachers or other adults. Rather, they preferred to say, "talking about the future" or "talking about what they were going to do when they leave school." In addition to variation among the youth, there was also variation in the way teachers used the word career. Some used it broadly to describe a life process, while others used it to talk about a next step they might take.

For us, this raises an important question: *How can we develop a common understanding of career and key career-related vocabulary and terminology?* Career is a complex term to understand and define. Helpfully, research and scholarship combined with the work of career development organizations provides insight from which we can begin to build a common understanding. Let's begin by reviewing what CERIC says about career:

> *"A lifestyle concept that involves the sequence of occupations (paid and unpaid) in which one engages throughout a lifetime, including work, learning, and leisure activities."* (CERIC, n.d.)

This definition distinguishes *career* from an *occupation*. This distinction is also shared by the National Career Development Association who differentiate *career* from *occupation* in their definition:

> *"Career is a more encompassing term that includes, but is not limited to, the series of occupations one might expect to hold in the course of his or her working history."* (NCDA, 2011, p. 1)

The Career Development Institute (CDI) in the United Kingdom (UK) also offer an understanding of the term that recognizes the relationship between life and work:

> *"A career refers primarily to the sequence and variety of work roles, paid or unpaid, that individuals undertake throughout their lives; but it is also the construct which enables individuals to make sense of valued work opportunities and how their work roles relate to their wider life roles."* (CDI, 2017, p. 1)

Much like the definition provided by CERIC, CDI's definition of career as a *narrative* consisting of how individuals make *progress* through their lives combined with how they *make sense of that progression* and relate it to their other life roles. Scholarly researchers also agree that career is a narrative and a journey.

In this toolkit, we adopt CERIC's conceptualization of career and utilize a slightly abbreviated version of their definition, defining career as:

A lifelong journey of learning about oneself and the individual interactions you have with learning, work, and life experiences.

This definition embraces the view that an individual's career is made up of a series of transitions, some of which are planned (e.g., attending college or university) or unplanned (e.g., unexpected job loss). We adopt this understanding and definition of career not only because CERIC's work is grounded within the Canadian context, but also because it is consistent with other expert-developed definitions of career (e.g., Andrews & Hooley, 2023; Cahill & Furey, 2017; Watts, 2004).

Let's pause our journey...

What does the term career mean to you?

How would you describe your understanding of this important term to a student, colleague, or parent?

If you were to choose a metaphor to explain your understanding of career, what would that metaphor be?

Conceptualizing and visualizing career: A lifespan perspective

To further refine these definitions, we consider how CERIC's (n.d.) Guiding Principles of Career Development recognizes career development as a lifelong process or journey:

"A career is about the life you want to lead – not just a job, occupation or profession. It involves deciding among possible and preferred futures. It answers: 'Who do I want to be in the world?' 'What kind of lifestyle am I seeking?' and 'How can I make an impact?'"

This is a useful pointer to the work of Super (1980) who described career in terms of "The Life Career Rainbow," illuminating the different life stages that a person goes through and how career development is embodied within each stage. Within this framework, career is defined as "the combination and sequence of roles played by a person during the course of a lifetime" (p. 282), with the first role being that of childhood.

Childhood is an important time during which children begin to think about the future. It is during this phase of life that people develop personal autonomy, a commitment to learning, and the competencies that will help them be successful in life. This process of growth reinforces children's confidence and their ability to work collaboratively with others, while developing a healthy competitive nature. Towards the end of this stage, children become more engaged in thinking about their long-term futures.

Within the childhood life stage, Super (1980) sets out several key concepts:

- **Growth:** Children are continuously growing and changing physically, cognitively, and socially, which affects their attitudes and expectations toward work.
- **Developmental tasks:** Children have specific developmental tasks that they need to achieve as they progress through different stages of childhood, such as acquiring basic skills, developing a sense of identity, and establishing relationships with peers.
- **Curiosity:** Children are naturally curious and have a desire to explore and learn about the world around them, including the world of work. Encouraging children's curiosity about different careers can help them develop career interests and aspirations.

These concepts provide a foundation for understanding career development in childhood and can be used by parents, educators, and other adults to support children's career development. It is important to note that these concepts are interrelated and continue to influence career development throughout the lifespan.

Super (1980) helps us understand that the way in which someone conceptualizes career can depend on multiple factors such as age, gender, culture, and ability or disability. For some people from equity seeking or socially disadvantaged groups, career can be seen as only relating to those who are working and are employed (Wilson & Jackson, 1998). This perspective can be limiting and can result in low expectations of self and others. The idea that a career is only associated with work that generates an income is restrictive, as voluntary activity and specialist learning also provides valuable sources of life satisfaction and contributes to overall community and societal well-being found through career.

Using metaphors to visualize career

One approach to understanding and visualizing career is to use metaphors (e.g., Amundson, 2010; McIlveen & Creed, 2018). For example, Inkson and Amundson (2002) identified 10 archetypal metaphors:

- Career as journey
- Career as inheritance
- Career as (good or bad) fit
- Career as a sequence of seasons

- Career as growth
- Career as a creative work
- Career as a network
- Career as a resource
- Career as a story
- Career as a cultural artefact

As illustrated in these examples, metaphors provide a way to make the abstract concept of career more tangible and meaningful to the individual. Five of Inkson and Amundson's metaphors are of particular interest and relevance to work with elementary school children:

Career as a journey: This metaphor sees career development as a journey, with twists and turns, detours, and unexpected events. It emphasizes the importance of adaptability and resilience in responding to changing circumstances.

Career as a story: This metaphor emphasizes the narrative aspect of career development, with individuals constructing their own life stories through the choices they make and the experiences they have.

Career as growth: This metaphor suggests that career represents an opportunity for individuals to learn, change and develop. Career is seen as way of an individual expressing their potential. In this metaphor, change and growth are seen as an integration of personal growth and development in home and work.

Career as fit: This metaphor emphasizes the relationship between an individual's characteristics and the roles they wish to pursue. The metaphor raises questions about the extent to which we can match people to jobs.

Career as a cultural artefact: This metaphor recognizes that there are cultural influences on the way people conceive of and enact their careers. It suggests that those supporting others in their career thinking should be open to the different possibilities that alternative cultural influences bring to the process and to suspend their own cultural assumptions.

Like the ideas shared by Inkson and Amundson (2002), CERIC (n.d.) utilizes the metaphor of a canoe to represent "our careers – we use it on our journey, we stock it with the tools we need, and we proactively steer it to our destination." Comparable metaphors appear in French language literature (e.g., Cohen-Scali et al., 2018), and Moore and Hooley (2012) noted that each metaphor names and conceptualizes career in a different way.

Law (2008) argued that using metaphors to conceptualize career can impact how individuals come to view and understand career. For example, visualizing career as a race versus a journey places career into a competitive mindset. Law argued that when career is conceptualized as a race, it implies a competitive process. However, when the notion of *journey* is applied (turning points, horizon, travel, and map), a different set of concepts and values are conveyed.

The way in which an individual conceptualizes career can also impact their expectations of career support in later life. For instance, if your view of career is as a race, you are more likely to seek out a career coach as someone who can help you be more competitive and get ahead. If your view of career is as a journey, then you are more likely to seek out someone who can guide you and make you aware of the different options available.

Understanding additional career-related vocabulary and terminology

Career is just one term that is helpful in engaging young learners in career-related learning conversations. When talking about career, we use a lot of words and phrases to describe individual's options, expectations, or outcomes. Young learners will often develop an understanding of these words through exposure to the word career through their communities, families, and the media (Cahill & Furey, 2017).

Some children will know that their parents *go to work* but may not fully understand what that entails. Others may live in a family where no one currently works, a community where there are limited work options, or a community dominated by one industry. Subsequently, children's understanding of the term *work* will vary. Some children may hear older siblings talk about educational options, such as university or college, but have no understanding of what these organizations are, and some children will have a much deeper understanding of secondary school and post-secondary options.

There are many examples of different career-related words in common use that are useful for children to understand. For example, Moore and Hooley (2012) identified ten career-related words used on the internet in career resources or websites including work, job, skills, training, college, sixth form (a special kind of college in England), apprenticeship, qualifications, university, and industry. When they questioned young people's understanding of these terms, they discovered a lack of consistency of definition and understanding.

Moving beyond colonialist understandings of career

Our schools are increasingly comprised of students who have various family structures, cultural norms, habits, and preferences. A broad and flexible approach should be undertaken when exploring terminology. We have highlighted some commonly held conceptions of career-related terms, words, and phrases and we acknowledge that many of these are rooted in colonialist understandings of career. A useful resource to help you begin to undertake a broader and more inclusive approach in your career-related terminology work are the *Guiding Circles* publications produced by Indigenous Works (formerly the Aboriginal Human Resource Council). *Guiding Circles* conceptualises career as a circle, like the medicine wheel. It can be used to help students to see and understand the gifts that are within them and make decisions about how to best use those gifts. Importantly, terminology used in the publications relates to family, life roles and responsibilities, connections, balance, values, personal style, and spirit. We encourage you to investigate such resources to help you broaden the range of career-related terminology you explore with your students.

Key findings from our study

In this section, we share some important findings from our study that relate to talking about careers. We begin by sharing data from educators, followed by students' perceptions, and finally the perspectives of parents and carers.

What does the term "career" mean to educators?

When asked to define the term "career," educators came up with descriptions that were well aligned with conceptions of career articulated by career experts. Sample responses included:

"Your whole body of work"

"A vocation to which one feels a commitment beyond just toiling through the dailyness of a job - often involves ongoing training/education and interest in engaging beyond just showing up every day"

"A career is the variety of experiences that you have undertaken throughout your life. As you gain more experience in the worlds of work and life, you are building your career. Your career path takes account of your education, training and paid or unpaid work. It also includes your family and life roles, activities, volunteer work, community involvement and more."

As can be seen, these responses present a holistic view of career and one that goes beyond a job.

How are grade 4 to 6 educators teaching about careers?

When asked what specific actions they have taken to teach students about careers, respondents gave a variety of answers. The most common was showing videos (especially on YouTube) followed by inviting guest speakers into the class. Other strategies included field trips, research projects, using resources (such as books, websites, or posters), and even role play. We saw no evident patterns in the data regarding who used what strategies and are assuming that these are individual choices made depending on teacher preferences, availability of resources, and professional judgements about what works best for students.

Educators reported that students ask about a variety of jobs. Consistent with prior research, these jobs tend to be ones that students have some experience with or knowledge of. Examples include teacher, nurse, doctor, professional athlete, actor, singer, YouTuber, or a job that a parent or family member has. Students cannot ask about jobs they do not know exist and so this finding highlights the need to expose students to potential jobs, industries, and career paths that may not be obvious to them.

What does the term "career" mean to pre-service teachers?

When asked to define the term "career," 79% of pre-service teachers came up with descriptions that focused on jobs or paid work. Sample responses included:

"Employment"

"A career is a commitment to a job (field of employment) that people hold for several years"

"The thing you get up and do everyday to earn a living"

The other responses were more aligned with a holistic view of career and one that goes beyond a job. Samples of those responses include:

"A way to build passions into your community contributions in an ongoing way"

"Career is a passion that is fulfilled through aligning interests with compensation"

Compared to practicing educators, pre-service teachers focused more on the paid employment aspect of career. This likely reflects differences in life stages and experience as the sample of educators were mostly over 40-years-old and pre-service teachers are typically in their early twenties.

The finding that pre-service teachers viewed "career" primarily as paid employment while practicing teachers had a more holistic definition of career may explain why pre-service teachers had lower levels of support for career education in grades 4 to 6. It is unreasonable to expect students in elementary school to be selecting or preparing for specific jobs, and so if one defines "career" as a specific paid job, then it follows that career education in grades 4 to 6 would be viewed as unreasonable.

What does the term "career" mean to students in grades 4–6?

When students were asked to define "career" two thirds of them wrote "job" or something similar. Sample responses included:

"Job"

"A job"

"A long-term job"

There were some more sophisticated responses such as:

"When I hear the word career I think of a job. A job/profession by someone that has helped them build a good life and they're so good at it"

As well as responses that clearly related to jobs but did not use that word. One example was:

"An office"

Compared to the educators, students had a simplistic view of career, indicating this is an area where career-related education could be helpful to students in grades 4 to 6.

Who do grade 4 to 6 students talk to about careers? What jobs do they talk about?

Our student respondents indicated they talk little about careers or future jobs. Only three respondents reported talking about careers "Quite often" and these discussions were had with friends or parents—not teachers. This contrasts with the educator survey where educators reported frequent classroom conversations about jobs and careers. When students reported talking about careers, it was almost always with friends or parents and rarely with teachers.

Not all respondents indicated what types of jobs they talk about, but among those that did half of them indicated jobs related to technology (e.g., computer programmer). Sometimes the language was vague (e.g., *"computer coding guy"*) but it was clear that grade 4 to 6 students understand the technology sector is an area where employment opportunities exist. Other jobs mentioned included familiar jobs such as teacher, police officer, actress, and veterinarian. This finding was consistent with the data obtained from the educator survey.

Another item in the survey asked respondents how often their parents talk to them about their jobs and 75% of respondents indicated that parents speak to them every day about their work. This would explain the finding in the educator survey that students know about, and will speak about, the jobs their parents have. Consistent with this was the finding that half of the student respondents visit a parental workplace every day or almost every day.

What does the term "career" mean to parents?

When asked to define the term "career," parents (like educators) came up with descriptions that were well aligned with conceptions of career articulated by career experts. Sample responses included:

> *"A journey of work and play and self-growth"*

> *"All aspects of life: from education and employment to family and community life"*

> *"Job, education, and community involvement"*

There were some responses that focused on work only, such as:

> *"The work one does"*

> *"Something you do throughout your life to make money"*

But most responses offered a holistic view of career that included work, education, and community involvement. It would appear from our data that educators and parents share similar conceptions of career and that notions of career are developed over time into adulthood.

What do parents report about the jobs their children talk about?

When parents were asked what jobs their children talk about, approximately one third of respondents (32%) said their children did not ask about or talk about jobs with them. This is consistent with an earlier item on the survey where 71% of parents said they talk about jobs with their child(ren). When job related discussions do happen, parents reported a broader range of jobs than educators or students did on their surveys. The parent survey included jobs we saw on the student surveys (e.g., veterinarian, YouTuber, police officer, teacher) but other jobs were mentioned we did not see on the student surveys (e.g., accountant, counselling psychology, engineer, farmer, prosecutor, trades, business owner). Some parents noted that they talk about their own job with their child(ren) and it is possible that these discussions led to the broader range of jobs mentioned in the survey responses. Thirty percent (30%) of parent respondents said they had been asked by their child's teacher to come to the school to discuss their work/job with the class.

Let's pause our journey...

What career-related words and terminology do you frequently use?

How do you define them?

How might a ten-year-old understand these words and terms?

Experiencing the journey: How does this chapter come to life in my classroom?

Implications for practice

For elementary educators, there are important points and implications for practice that emerge from an examination of terminology, vocabulary, and what it means to talk about careers. For example, those tasked with leading discussions about and the formal teaching and learning of careers need to keep in mind that the concept of *career* is more than an occupation and encompasses one's life journey. Thus, a classroom discussion of a term like *work* should include the different ways the term is used. Some examples might be paid work, schoolwork, voluntary work, or working to repair a relationship. Similarly, recognizing the lifespan perspective reminds educators that even when they are not specifically addressing career-related learning in practice (e.g., lesson designed to address a career-related curriculum expectation), daily experiences, activities, and interactions within the classroom, school, and playground all contribute to early understanding of career.

Law (1996) noted that career development is a process that can be taught. This awareness does not suggest that elementary teachers should be encouraging learners to make early choices about jobs, but rather that learners can thoughtfully and purposefully be introduced to common and useful vocabulary, terminology, and concepts that are fundamental in supporting the ongoing career-related learning and conversations.

For any conversation about career-related terminology to be meaningful and productive, there must be agreement on what it is you are talking about. Thus, it is vital that educators, children, and career influencers share common definitions of key terms. This realization raises several questions for educators tasked with exploring the delivery of careers education and learning, including:

- What words and ideas do students need to learn?
- When should educators begin to have career conversations with elementary students?
- What opportunities exist for students to use and develop these career-related terms?

What words and ideas do students need to learn?

Being able to effectively talk about careers with elementary age learners requires a common language and understanding. Before an exchange of ideas can begin, educators may need to consider and reflect on the question, *what words and terms do young learners in my school need to know (and be able to use fluently) to engage in meaningful and productive career-related discussions and conversations?*

The answer to this question is not straight forward. Although there are some standard words that are used widely, such as *career, job*, and *work*, other key terms will vary depending on socio-cultural factors. The community or region where these discussions are taking place will influence the words and vocabulary used. Similarly, guiding curriculum frameworks and documents will inform the adoption and utilization of key terms and vocabulary within career conversations at school. For instance, whereas an emphasis is placed on developing *skills* within Ontario, the term *competencies* is used within Quebec. In other parts of the country, both terms are used (e.g., British Columbia).

Recognizing this variation, it is important that educators refer to relevant curriculum documents and frameworks for guidance when identifying words and ideas to focus on within career-related conversations. In addition, educators are encouraged to undertake some research of their own to identify the key words and terminology relevant to their community of practice.

Let's pause our journey...

What approaches could you use to learn about the preferred use of vocabulary with your community? Here are some examples:

- A survey for parents

- Using mind maps with parents, students, and teachers

- Create a professional learning community with your teacher colleagues

- Create a game that students can play in class.

A helpful online vocabulary and terminology resource is CERIC's *Glossary of Career Development*. Created by CERIC and the Canadian Council for Career Development (CCCD), this glossary is intended to serve as a resource for those engaging in career-related work and learning and for those seeking definitions of terms (see resources and further reading section of this chapter). In Table 4, we have adapted some examples from CERIC's Glossary of Career Development as a sample of how these terms relate to the elementary school setting. Having access to this Glossary of Career Development is a useful starting point to help you to explore a wide range of career-related terms with your students.

Table 4.

Career, job, and work as defined within CERIC's glossary of career development

Career	Career is a lifestyle concept and includes a sequence of learning, leisure and paid and unpaid work that you might engage in over a lifetime. Seeing a career in this way allows us to understand our relationship with work at a personal level. Exploring the individual relationship with work—especially through values, talents and goals—gives us a better chance of making it a success.
Job	A job is a paid or unpaid position that requires us to use our knowledge, experiences and skills to help us perform tasks and activities, usually within an organization or business. A job can be parttime, full-time, temporary, or permanent. We may have one or more jobs, and we usually have more than one job over a lifetime.
Work	Work is a set of activities with an intended set of outcomes, from which it is hoped that we gain personal satisfaction and fulfilment, and we hope will help us feel a sense of contributing to some greater goal. Work may not be tied to a paid job, but it does describe our participation in meaningful and satisfying activities, (e.g., volunteer work, hobbies).

When should we have career conversations with elementary students?

When thinking about your career-related learning conversations with students, you may wonder if elementary school is too early to begin thinking and talking about careers.

As we and others have argued, career development is a lifelong process that begins in the early years and develops over time. In the elementary school context, engaging in career conversations is not about getting children to make decisions about what job they will have in the future. Rather, it is a time when we ask our young learners to begin the process of investigating themselves, find out more about their interests and aptitudes, and consider what type of life they feel they might want to lead. This means thinking about questions like: what do I like to do most? what do I think I am good at? what makes me happy? and how can I best help others?

CERIC (n.d.) illuminates that career development is something that entails identifying and exploring personal interests, beliefs, values, skills, and competencies and is supported by educators, family members, peers, and other members of the community. Cahill and Furey (2017) also asserted that:

> *"...children actively explore their worlds and begin to construct possibilities for present and future selves. These life stories include a sense of self (self-identity), life roles, skills, and knowledge, and are shaped by everyday events and experiences, as well as by interests, attitudes, beliefs, and role models."* (p. 12)

Cahill and Furey highlighted how the "seeds of career development" (p. 6) are already planted and beginning to develop in the early years among children aged three- to eight-years-old. Indeed, according to Cahill and Furey, parents have noted that from a very young age, children will share ideas about growing up and their hopes and dreams

for the future. Concludingly, educators have realized that it is never too early to talk about career as both career choice and career decision-making are complex and ongoing processes.

We know that children model behaviours and learn lessons about their environments through contact with and emersion into different situations, contexts, and environments. Some of these lessons may be valuable. However, we also know that where children's understanding of the world can be narrowly defined and limited, which in turn can limit aspiration and opportunity, resulting in a lifetime of poverty and disadvantage (e.g., Hartung et al., 2005; Sellers et al., 1999; Watson & McMahon, 2005). From an early age, children need to engage in career-related learning, begin to develop career literacy, and engage in career-related conversations to make sense of their options and to raise their ambition (Perry et al., 2016). Helping educators understand that they have a role to play within this process is an important first step.

What opportunities are there for students to develop their understanding and application of career-related terms?

To help you think about curriculum activities that enhance understanding and use of career-related terminology, it is important to understand the extent to which you currently hold career-related conversations with your students:

- Are these informal or formal conversations?
- What stimulates these conversations?
- Do they involve parents or other community members? (e.g., sport coaches or music teachers)
- How confident do you feel when you are called upon to have career-related conversations?

It is only by understanding the answers to these questions that we can begin to develop formal and informal curriculum responses. The answers will also help you formulate any training and development activities for the staff and teachers in your school.

Let's pause our journey...

Do you have a career-related learning champion in your school?

Having a career-related learning champion can help support meaningful and authentic career-related conversations and teaching and learning experiences within your school. This individual might undertake the following:

1. Gather information to understand how career-related words and terminology are understood in your context.

2. Provide training for staff to help them to understand the rationale for the task and to give them an opportunity to develop an approach. This can involve sharing some of the examples in this section.

3. Create a curriculum map of where career-related vocabulary learning can take place.

Example activities for you to think about

In the next section of this toolkit, you will find a selection of activities to help you incorporate some of the concepts in this chapter into your teaching practice. Note that you can use these activities as they are presented or adapt them to suit your individual learning environment.

Activity:
Careers Terminology Music Quiz

Aim: This activity helps students to increase their knowledge on the range of jobs and enforces how words associated with jobs are incorporated into all aspects of popular culture.

Activity Description: There are numerous songs that feature different jobs, either in the main body of the song or in the song titles. These can be played in-class as a short fun activity and students can see how many jobs they can spot.

Here are some suggested songs to get you started...

Tiny Dancer - Elton John	Please Mr. Postman – The Marvelettes
Paperback writer – The Beatles	Teacher I Need You – Elton John
The Scientist – Coldplay	Coal Miner's Daughter – Loretta Lynn
Space Oddity – David Bowie	Mr. Telephone Man – New Edition
Photograph – Ed Sheeran	Paparazzi – Lady Gaga
Rockstar – Nickelback	Watching the Detectives – Elvis Costello
Karma Police – Radiohead	The Boxer – Simon & Garfunkel
Monkey Wrench – Foo Fighters	Rhinestone Cowboy – Glen Campbell
Bartender – James Blunt	Piano Man – Billy Joel
Doctor Doctor – Thompson Twins	Rock DJ – Robbie Williams

Career Connections:

This activity can be adapted where the entire class tries to find songs with job titles in them. To take the activity further, students could also be asked to identify tasks and activities associated with jobs that are reflected in the songs

Activity:
Developing metaphors

(adapted from Metaphor Making by Norm Amundson)

Aim: To develop students understanding of how to use metaphors to explore ideas related to career

Activity Description:

1. Prior to working with metaphors, it is important to establish that your students understand what a metaphor is. This activity is a good opportunity to check their understanding.
2. To begin this activity, you might share the following 2–3 examples of a metaphor that is commonly associated with career.

   Climbing the Ladder of Success

   The Journey

   Career Anchors

3. Either individually or in small groups, students can select one of these metaphors and share their thoughts on what the metaphor is saying about career. You may need to prompt them at various points in their discussion.
4. Still working individually or in small groups, students can then create their own metaphors and share these with the rest of the class.
5. Students can either write or draw these metaphors.
6. To support students in their thinking, you can share with them various career-related terminology they already have some familiarity with.

Career Connections:

Metaphorical thinking — our instinct not just for describing but for comprehending one thing in terms of another, for equating one concept with another — shapes our view of the world, and is essential to how we communicate, learn, discover, and invent. Therefore, metaphors are very useful in career-related activities, and we encourage you to be creative in how you approach working with metaphors. The world is your oyster!

Activity:
Drawing a career

Aim: To help students explore common misconceptions about different jobs

Activity Description:

1. Ask students to draw a picture of a job they think they will do in the future, and/or ask students to draw themselves doing a job they think they would like to do.
2. Each variation of this activity can raise different discussions. The first variance will help you to learn more about what students' aspirations and knowledge of what jobs might be available. This activity can also raise important discussions about stereotyping jobs.
3. The second variance helps to unpack what tasks and activities students are associating with jobs. This activity helps students to think through what types of tasks and activities are interesting to them.
4. Drawing activities could be undertaken with pens, pencils and paint, or digitally with a suitable software program.
5. Once students have completed their drawings, you can lead a discussion about the images students have chosen. You might like to explore where students have got their ideas from (e.g., parents, friends, social media, watching television shows), and you might also like to repeat the drawing exercise over time to see if students' perceptions change. This can be especially useful after you have engaged in a period of career-related learning to investigate impact on students.

Note: This activity can be adapted in many ways. For example, you could ask students to draw people working in specific occupations or jobs such as engineering, medicine, education or farmers, emergency service workers, serving staff etc. Such activities can be helpful in exploring students' understandings of who typically works in such fields or industries, and the types of work they undertake.

Career Connections:

Drawing-based activities can be used to provide students with opportunities to think about their skills, values, and interests in a holistic and creative way. Furthermore, such activities encourage students to develop their self-reflective skills, which are essential for lifelong learning throughout one's career. Many different creative learning activities facilitate career exploration, including collaborative drawing, story boarding, photovoice, creative writing, video, sculpting and textile weaving. Using creative learning for career-related learning does not have to be costly. Inexpensive art materials can be used to great effect!

Additional resources to support your activities:

- **Canva:** a free storyboard tool that includes templates, images, icons, stickers and graphics as well options for students to upload their own photos, images and art.
- **Miro:** a free online whiteboard including templates, the ability to add images and files, and the possibility of integrating with other tools.
- **Storyboard That:** a drag-and-drop creation platform offering simple and helpful visual tools.

Activity:
Exploring career-related terms with Frayer Diagrams

Aim: The Frayer diagram (Frayer et al., 1969) is a visual learning tool used to help students understand and remember new vocabulary words or concepts. It was developed by Dorothy Frayer and her colleagues at the University of Wisconsin in the 1960s.

Activity Description: The diagram consists of a four-quadrant box with the vocabulary word or concept in the centre, and four sections around it. The four sections are labeled *Definition*, *Characteristics*, *Examples*, and *Non-Examples*.

My Definition	Characteristics
Example	Picture to Describe

The *Definition* section requires students to provide a clear and concise definition of the word or concept in their own words. The *Characteristics* section asks students to list the key attributes or qualities of the word or concept. The *Examples* section asks students to provide specific examples that illustrate the word or concept, while the *Non-Examples* section asks students to provide examples that are not related to the word or concept but may be confused with it.

Career Connections:

The Frayer diagram is often used in language arts, science, and social studies classes, and can be adapted for use in any subject area. It helps students develop their critical thinking and vocabulary acquisition skills by requiring them to analyze and synthesize information in a visual and organized manner.

Evaluating the journey: How do I know this is worthwhile?

The fact that you are reading this toolkit suggests that you have an interest in career-related learning within the elementary school context. It may be that you already have some training in this area or it may be that these concepts and ideas are entirely new to you. Wherever you are in you are in your learning journey, identifying your knowledge and skills gaps and planning your own program of professional development will be an important element in your success.

Let's pause our journey...

What is your understanding of the term *career*?

What influences this view?

How does this influence the conversations that you might have with both staff and students in your school?

You might want to keep a reflective journal to record your thoughts as they develop.

As you undertake career-related activities in your own learning contexts and environments, consider building in some ways to evaluate the effectiveness of your journey. Through evaluation you can think more deeply about your journey, identifying what you have done, what has gone well, and what you might do differently next time round. Importantly, evaluation can help you to determine whether you achieved what you set out to do, and what impact your career-related teaching is having on your young learners.

Journey reflections: Key takeaways

Career is a complex term with multiple definitions and understandings. The variances of interpretation and understanding can complicate conversations and cause confusion as to what career-related learning is really about.

Career-related vocabulary and terminology are the building blocks to effective career research and conversations. Elementary aged students are ready to benefit from such conversations.

Childhood is an important time during which children begin to think about the future. It is during this phase of life that people develop personal autonomy, a commitment to learning, and the competencies that will help them be successful in life.

Metaphors provide a way to make the abstract concept of career more tangible and meaningful and provide a fun and creative way for students to explore what career and career-related learning terminology means to them.

From an early age, children need to engage in career-related learning, begin to develop career literacy, and engage in career-related conversations to make sense of their options and to raise their ambition. Educators have an important role to play within this process.

Chapter 3
Nurturing and Developing Foundational Skills

Exploring the possibilities: What is this chapter about?

This chapter focuses on how schools and educators can help children develop foundational skills that are critical for success in life. For decades now, educators have understood that schools need to do more than just teach content and facts. Classroom teachers help children develop skills that underpin not only their academic success but their success in life as well. Thus, we see educators striving to help students become better collaborators, enhance creativity, persevere in the face of challenges, and use technology effectively and ethically. Of course, this list of skills is not complete. There are myriad skills people need to engage with and navigate the world successfully. Even the lists provided within this chapter are not exhaustive, but they help to illustrate the breadth and depth of skills needed not only for individual success across the lifespan but also for a cohesive Canadian society. Those specializing in career development and education refer to these skills as *career-related skills*, but many educators and parents think of them as *life skills*, *essential skills*, or *foundational skills*.

Take collaboration as an example. Almost all jobs require teamwork. There are very few human endeavours that are individual efforts. Whether it is building a house, creating a legal argument, or developing software, the world of work is a world of teamwork. Teachers understand that collaborative skills are valuable in all areas of life and so they assign group projects and collaborative tasks.

As we have noted, "career" is an encompassing term that goes beyond paid work. Collaboration is a critical skill not just in school or in the workplace but in many areas of our lives. For instance, children collaborate as part of their play, educators collaborate to help children learn, and families collaborate in creating a life together.

The argument made about the widespread importance of collaboration is not limited to this one skill. All the skills listed within this chapter (and many more that we have not mentioned) have widespread utility in our lives. For example, we need to be effective questioners to understand tasks and the perspectives of others, digital skills to navigate the modern world, and emotional intelligence for our own happiness and well-being.

The need for schools to develop skills in children is broadly accepted. Merchant et al. (2018) found that every provincial school system in Canada asks teachers to develop and assess skills beyond academic achievement, with the most commonly assessed skills being collaboration, responsibility, organization, and the ability to work independently. The rationale for including the development and assessment of skills in schools includes economic reasons (e.g., personal success and economic contributions to society), personal reasons (e.g., supporting lifelong learning and personal fulfillment), and social reasons (e.g., contributing to society).

Why should I be reading this chapter?

Elementary educators know that the most enduring and important learning from those years often relates to foundational skills. Obviously, literacy and numeracy are foundational skills, but other important skills are developed in elementary school too. Reading this chapter will give you a sampling of what skills are important for students' current and future lives, alongside some concrete ideas about how to develop and assess these skills in practice.

Planning and packing for the journey: What do I need to be thinking about?

Elementary educators reading this chapter may find that the ideas presented align with their current practice. We recognize the fantastic work already being done in Canadian schools to help children develop foundational skills that will be useful in their futures. Thus, as you read this chapter, think about how the ideas presented here relate to your current teaching and how they may extend your practice.

What are foundational skills?

Foundational skills are synonymous with career-related skills, essential skills, and life skills. CERIC (n.d.) suggests that essential skills are those "needed for work, learning and other activities of daily life. They provide the foundation for learning all other skills, such as technical skills, and enable people to evolve with their jobs and adapt to change." Thus, when we refer to foundational skills, we are talking about these career-related, essential, life skills – skills that are already being developed in schools. Examples of such skills include literacy, numeracy, problem-solving, and collaboration.

What skills should be developed in elementary school?

Many different skills are useful in school, work, and everyday life. We see this notion reflected by the large number skills that school systems aim to develop. Merchant et al. (2018) found over 20 different skills appear on Canadian report cards across the country. Internationally, similar lists of skills are emphasized and developed in schools. For example, Singapore (2023) includes character development, cooperative skills, and self-management skills as part of its education system. The European Union (2019) created a list of key competencies that included literacy and numeracy, the ability to work with digital technologies, creativity, entrepreneurship, and civic mindedness. Indeed, it is rare to find a school system anywhere in the world that does not aim to develop skills beyond academic achievement.

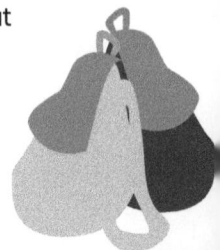

In our own research, we asked elementary educators, pre-service teachers, parents, and business/industry people to name the most important skill to be developed in grade 4 to 6 classrooms. The top five responses for each group of people are shown in Table 5.

Table 5.
Most important skills to be developed in grade 4 to 6 classrooms by group of survey respondents.

Rank	Educators	Pre-service teachers	Parents	Business/ Industry
1	writing	self-regulation	communication	responsibility
2	communication	communication	writing	reading
3	self-regulation	writing	problem solving	communication
4	creativity and innovation	collaboration	collaboration	self-regulation
5	collaboration	responsibility	emotional intelligence	creativity and innovation

Notably, no single skill was a runaway favourite. Each group of respondents valued multiple skills and saw them as important to develop in the classroom.

With regards to exactly what skills should be developed in elementary school, there is no single answer and there does not need to be. Educators know that students have unique and varied strengths and needs. Moreover, diverse communities and cultures impart different values to skills (e.g., collaboration vs. working independently). And so, the question of what skills should be developed in school is one that is best addressed at the local level. Looking forward in the document, the learning principles outlined in Table 9 come from an indigenous perspective whereas the ones in Table 7 reflect pan-European circumstances. Your own teaching context is unique, and we encourage you to select skills that are most germane to your professional situation.

Childhood and adolescence are vital life stages when it comes to learning essential skills. Thus, we see school systems and teachers focus on a wide array of skills, such as:

- Academic skills, such as reading, writing, and numeracy;
- Personal skills such as self-regulation, responsibility, and healthy habits;
- Social and emotional skills, such as identifying and managing emotions, critical and creative thinking, and healthy relationships; and
- Technical skills, such as digital literacy and the use of information technology.

To help you better understand and explore essential skills, we present four frameworks and show how they relate to each other: (a) Skills for Success – Government of Canada; (b) Key Competences for Lifelong Learning – European Union; (c) SkillsUSA – United States of America; and (d) First Peoples' Principles of Learning. As you learn about these frameworks, notice that while each framework is different in content and scope, there is substantial overlap.

Framework #1: Skills for Success (Government of Canada)

Launched in 2021, the Government of Canada's Skills for Success framework outlines nine foundational skills "needed to participate and thrive in learning, work and life" (Government of Canada, 2023). A key understanding of this framework is that the Skills for Success are foundational for building additional skills and knowledge and essential for social interaction. Of note, these skills are not independent of one another. Rather, they "overlap and interact" and can be adapted to various contexts. For example, one cannot use digital tools effectively without also being a good reader. Similarly, being a good problem-solver requires creativity. In Table 6, you will find a list of the Skills for Success along with a description of each skill. As you review this list of skills, you may note that you already observe, address, and help students develop them in multiple ways in your classroom practice. As you read each description, it may be helpful to ask yourself: *In what ways do I support the development of this skill in my classroom?*

Elementary educators will recognize that all nine of these skills are currently being developed in Canada's elementary schools. Teachers assign collaborative assignments to groups of students, have them work with digital tools, and work hard to improve literacy and numeracy outcomes. It can sound jarring to talk about career-related skills in elementary school because these children are too young to be making concrete preparations for the world of work. However, career-related skills are also school skills, relationship skills, and civic skills—all of which elementary educators aim to develop in their students. These skills are career-related because they are useful in all areas of life, not because they are specific to careers or the world of work.

Table 6.

Government of Canada's Skills for Success Framework

Skills for Success (Government of Canada)	
Adaptability	Your ability to achieve or adjust goals and behaviours when expected or unexpected change occurs, by planning, staying focused, persisting, and overcoming setbacks. We use this skill to change work plans to meet new deadlines, learn how to work with new tools and improve our skills through feedback.
Collaboration	Your ability to contribute and support others to achieve a common goal. For example, at work we use this skill to provide meaningful support to team members while completing a project.
Communication	Your ability to receive, understand, consider, and share information and ideas through speaking, listening, and interacting with others. We use this skill to listen to instructions, serve customers and discuss ideas.
Creativity and Innovation	Your ability to imagine, develop, express, encourage, and apply ideas in ways that are novel, unexpected, or challenge existing methods and norms. We use this skill to discover better ways of doing things, develop new products, and deliver services in a new way.
Digital	Your ability to use digital technology and tools to find, manage, apply, create and share information and content. We use this skill to create spreadsheets, safely use social media, and securely make online purchases.
Numeracy	Your ability to find, understand, use, and report mathematical information presented through words, numbers, symbols, and graphics. We use this skill to perform calculations, manage budgets, analyze and model data and make estimations.
Problem Solving	Your ability to identify, analyze, propose solutions, and make decisions. Problem solving helps you to address issues, monitor success, and learn from the experience. We use this skill to make hiring decisions, select courses of action and troubleshoot technical failures.
Reading	Your ability to find, understand, and use information presented through words, symbols, and images. We use this skill to locate information on forms and drawings, and to read items such as emails, reports, news articles, blog posts and instructions.
Writing	Your ability to share information using written words, symbols, and images. We use this skill to fill out forms and applications, and write emails, reports, and social media posts.

Framework #2: Key Competences for Lifelong Learning (European Union)

The European Union (EU) is an interesting context because it contains so many different countries within it. Despite the various cultures and education systems, countries within the EU have come to a consensus on what skills should be developed in schools and labeled these skills Key Competences for Lifelong Learning (EU, 2019). These key competences "include knowledge, skills, and attitudes needed by all for personal fulfilment and development, employability, social inclusion and active citizenship."

In Table 7, you will find a list of the Key Competences for Lifelong Learning along with their descriptions. Comparing them to the Canadian Skills for Success, you will notice that there is substantial overlap between the frameworks. As an example, Canadian elementary schools have a strong focus on literacy and numeracy and these skills are included in the EU framework. The "multilingual competence" is one that is necessary in a multicultural context such as the EU, but we can see its utility in an officially bilingual country such as Canada. We could also see how some Canadian schools may define the learning of Indigenous languages as part of their multilingual competences.

The "entrepreneurship competence" is an interesting one because it encompasses different skills that are valued in Canadian school systems. For instance, Ontario teachers must assess and report upon students' initiative and Alberta specifically mentions "entrepreneurial spirit" as something it aims to develop within its education system. Some of the descriptors included in the entrepreneurship competence (e.g., critical thinking, problem solving, perseverance) are valued in Canadian schools just as they are in European schools.

Table 7.

Key Competences for Lifelong Learning (European Union)

Key Competences for Lifelong Learning (European Union)	
Literacy Competence	Literacy is the ability to identify, understand, express, create and interpret concepts, feelings, facts, and opinions in both oral and written forms, using visual, audio, and digital materials across disciplines and contexts. It implies the ability to communicate and connect effectively with others.
Multilingual Competence	This competence defines the ability to use different languages appropriately and effectively for communication.
Mathematical Competence	Mathematical competence is the ability to develop and apply mathematical thinking and insight to solve a range of problems in everyday situations.
Competence in Science, Technology, and Engineering	Competence in science refers to the ability and willingness to explain the natural world by making use of the body of knowledge and methodology employed, including observation and experimentation, in order to identify questions and to draw evidence-based conclusions. Competences in technology and engineering are applications of that knowledge and methodology in response to perceived human wants or needs.
Digital Competence	Digital competence involves the confident, critical, and responsible use of, and engagement with, digital technologies for learning, at work, and for participation in society.
Personal, Social, and Learning to Learn Competence	Personal, social, and learning to learn competence is the ability to reflect upon oneself, effectively manage time and information, work with others in a constructive way, remain resilient and manage one's own learning and career. It includes the ability to cope with uncertainty and complexity, learn to learn, support one's physical and emotional well-being, maintain physical and mental health, and to lead a health-conscious, future-oriented life, empathize and manage conflict in an inclusive and supportive context.
Citizenship Competence	Citizenship competence is the ability to act as responsible citizens and to fully participate in civic and social life, based on understanding of social, economic, legal, and political concepts and structures, as well as global developments and sustainability.
Entrepreneurship Competence	Entrepreneurship competence refers to the capacity to act upon opportunities and ideas, and to transform them into values for others. It is founded upon creativity, critical thinking and problem solving, taking initiative and perseverance and the ability to work collaboratively to plan and manage projects that have cultural, social or financial value.

Framework #3: SkillsUSA (United States of America)

SkillsUSA is an American framework targeted at kindergarten to grade 12 students. The framework has a focus on career and technical education, but many aspects of it are relevant to elementary education too. The skills contained within the framework are divided into three categories: personal, technical, and workplace.

In Table 8, you will find a list of skills from the SkillsUSA framework that are relevant to elementary education. Again, you will notice some similarities among the skills identified within the SkillsUSA framework, the EU Key Competences for Lifelong Learning, and the Canadian Skills for Success.

Table 8.

The SkillsUSA framework

SkillsUSA		
Personal Skills	**Technical Skills**	**Workplace Skills**
• Integrity • Work Ethic • Responsibility • Adaptability • Self-Motivation	• Computer Literacy • Safety and Health • Service Orientation	• Communication • Decision-Making • Teamwork • Multicultural Sensitivity and Awareness • Planning, Organization, and Management • Leadership

From an educators' perspective, there is no need for the three separate categories as these skills intersect and interact. For example, responsibility is listed as a personal skill, but it clearly relates to skills in the other two categories, such as safety and health, teamwork, and planning, organization, and management.

The SkillsUSA framework does not provide precise definitions of each skill, but it does provide sample behaviours that teachers could observe[1]. This approach can be useful when trying to assess or develop specific skills with students. For instance, the personal skill of integrity has behaviours such as "make choices consistent with my values" and "do what I say what I will do" associated with it. Responsibility is associated with the behaviours of submitting schoolwork on time, honouring commitments, and persevering with tasks. These behaviours can serve as a starting point for teachers to devise their own definitions and assessments of the skills and to anchor formative feedback given to students.

Framework #4: First Peoples' Principles of Learning

The fourth framework is not a skills framework per se but we wanted to include it for several reasons. Firstly, even though this framework focuses on principles of learning and not skills, the connection between the two is clear. Secondly, this framework was written by the First Nations Education Steering Committee (www.fnesc.ca) in British Columbia and is useful for demonstrating the cultural and contextual nature of skill frameworks. The principles are given in Table 9. A poster of these principles can be downloaded from the FNESC website at https://www.fnesc.ca/wp/wp-content/uploads/2015/09/PUB-LFP-POSTER-Principles-of-Learning-First-Peoples-poster-11x17.pdf.

---

1   Please go to LessonPlan-v1.pdf (skillsusa.org) for a complete list of behaviours associated with each skill.

Table 9.

First Peoples' Principles of Learning

Learning ultimately supports the well-being of the self, the family, the community, the land, the spirits, and the ancestors.

Learning is holistic, reflexive, reflective, experiential, and relational (focused on connectedness, on reciprocal relationships, and a sense of place).

Learning involves recognizing the consequences of one's actions.

Learning involves generational roles and responsibilities.

Learning recognizes the role of indigenous knowledge.

Learning is embedded in memory, history, and story.

Learning involves patience and time.

Learning requires exploration of one's identity.

Learning involves recognizing that some knowledge is sacred and only shared with permission and/or in certain situations.

Looking at the First Peoples' Principles of Learning we can see that some principles are cultural in nature and specific to the Indigenous context (e.g., Learning recognizes the role of indigenous knowledge), while others are easy to relate to Western skills frameworks. For instance, "Learning involves patience and time" would relate to notions of perseverance and grit, "Learning involves recognizing the consequences of one's actions" relates to responsibility, and "Learning requires exploration of one's identity" relates to self-knowledge.

Cultural differences in which skills are valued and why can be an interesting area for exploration. In Canadian classrooms, we strive towards helping students develop their appreciation for, and understanding of, diverse cultures and examining skills can provide a meaningful path towards intercultural understanding. Note that this can be done at a family level too. Different families value different skills for different reasons. Having students explore this aspect of their family life can help them better understand their own identity.

What skills should I focus on in my classroom?

Given the various frameworks we have explored, and the myriad skills people use to successfully navigate the world, you may find yourself asking: What skills should be the focus of classroom teachers? This is a question that only the teacher can answer.

A teacher in a French Immersion classroom may decide that it is appropriate to focus on multilingual communication and intercultural competence. A teacher in a different classroom may decide that students need to better develop their planning skills. While it is up to the teacher's professional judgment as to how much focus should be put on different skills, we advise against trying to focus on too many skills as you will likely find it challenging to explore or develop any skill effectively. Each skill mentioned in this chapter is complex and context dependent. Thus, you may find it more rewarding to place emphasis on exploring and developing fewer skills in deep and meaningful ways.

The good news is that because the skills in each framework are interdependent, focusing on even one skill leads to the development of others. Imagine a grade 5 classroom where the teacher decides to focus on responsibility. Being responsible can mean being responsible to and collaborating with members of a group, it involves good planning, emotional- and self-regulation, and effective communication. Thus, while the classroom may have a focus on responsibility, other key skills are also nurtured and developed. The interdependency of skills could be further explored in concept map activities with your students.

Experiencing the journey: How does this chapter come to life in my classroom?

From structured activities, such as lessons and planned experiences, to unstructured opportunities, such as free play and recess, teachers and schools support the development of foundational skills. While there are countless ways to target and address specific skills at school, it is important to recognize that—whether they are doing so intentionally or not—teachers already provide numerous opportunities for students to refine, practice, and advance foundational skills through their everyday practice. For example, a small group of students may draw on their communication, problem solving, collaboration, and social-emotional skills when deciding what game to play or resolving a conflict in the school yard. A child may exercise their reading, writing, and creativity skills when building a school project or poster. Students may utilize their critical thinking, digital literacy, and communication skills when researching and investigating a topic online.

Nurturing and developing skills with intention

Career-related learning and skills can be supported in the classroom and school through intentional teaching, learning, and assessment practices that incorporate a variety of teacher- and student-directed experiences. It can be helpful to imagine this approach along a continuum with explicit and structured activities on one end and emergent and unstructured activities on the other, with various practices and endeavours falling across the spectrum.

Recognizing that career development is an individual journey that is supported and shaped by others, including educators, family, and peers (CERIC, n.d.), students should not be viewed as passive recipients of knowledge, but instead as indispensable partners and co-creators of career-related learning experiences and skill development. With such an approach, educators should seek to amplify and integrate student voice whenever possible.

One such approach is through individual conversations. Teachers spend much time with students, but often little of that time is in a one-to-one setting where the teacher and student can have a conversation. Deliberately scheduling time for individual conversations with students can enhance relationships and allow the teacher to have a better understanding of the student perspective. Such conversations need a focus. For example, goal setting:

- Goal setting is a critical component of planning processes, self-regulation, and self-assessment. However, many students do not set goals for themselves at school and never think about what they want to accomplish while at school.

- Asking students to set goals gives them agency and direction in their learning and spurs important thought processes about what experiences and benefits the student wants out of school.
- Goal setting conversations need to be followed up with regular conversations about the student's progress in achieving their goals. These conversations do not need to be frequent (2 to 3 times per year is sufficient), but they need to happen so the students have a formal opportunity to reflect on their progress, whether their initial goals are still useful and relevant, and what they need to do to further.

There are many opportunities to incorporate student voice when it comes to skill development. Some other ideas are:

- List 10 important skills and ask students to select one skill to be the focus for the month;
- With the students, co-construct a rubric to assess a specific skill or set of related skills;
- Have students self-assess themselves on a skill (or variety of skills); and
- If you use reward systems (e.g., points for cleaning up, helping others, etc.) allow the students to have input into the system and the rewards.

Let's pause our journey...

What are some ways that you are already nurturing and developing foundational skills in your practice?

What are some ways that you might bring additional opportunities for skill development into your practice?

How might you empower students to be partners and co-creators on this learning journey?

Valuing play as an opportunity for skill development

One of the findings that emerged from the research conducted to create this toolkit was that grade 4 to 6 students saw play as critical to their development of skills, such as conflict resolution, collaboration, problem-solving, and adaptability. Interestingly, elementary teachers also saw unstructured play time as critical in the development of foundational skills.

These findings align with a wider understanding that play is critical to children's development, learning, and well-being, and to their "ability to thrive by helping them develop core skills (creative, social, physical, emotional and cognitive) that are critical drivers of success in adulthood" (Thomsen, 2021, para. 4). Through play, children practice, develop, and refine holistic skills, including cognitive, social, emotional, physical, and creative skills (Zosh et al., 2022).

> **The Right to Play**
> Article 31 of the United Nations Convention on the Rights of the Child (UNCRC) recognizes the child's right to rest, leisure, play, and culture (UNICEF, n.d.; see also IPA World, 2013).
> Canada signed the UNCRC in 1991 and, by doing so, made a promise to protect and promote the rights outlined within it (Government of Canada, 2021).

Given the importance of play, the extent to which it is supported (and respected) within the classroom and school merits careful thought and consideration. Students generally have unstructured play time built into the school day through recess and lunch. However, recognizing that play is a critical time for skill development, teachers may realize that play ought to be incorporated into class time as well. Some possible strategies include:

- **Free Play!** Students are given the time and space to engage in self-guided play. Students can play alone or with friends, inside or outside. Try incorporating loose parts to see what students do with the material.
- **Learn what you want!** Students are given time to pursue learning anything they want (within acceptable and safe boundaries). This might be watching science videos on YouTube, learning cheat codes for video games, how to draw cartoon characters, etc.
- **Create a game!** Students work in groups to create a game (could be a board game, physical game, etc.) and then teach others how to play the game they have invented.
- **Puzzle time!** Students are given a choice of different puzzles to solve. These could be manipulative puzzles, logic puzzles, word games, Sudoku, etc.

Student self-assessment

Skills are an excellent opportunity for incorporating student self-assessment into your practice. In fact, many teachers do this already (Merchant et al., 2022). The reason self-assessment works so well for skills such as responsibility or adaptability is because some aspects of those skills are not visible to the teacher. For instance, a student may be doing work at home to ensure they have all their assignments completed or may have faced difficulties you were not aware of in completing a project. By asking students to self-assess their skills, you are opening an important conversation about their learning, self-concept, and how they hope to improve. Here are a few ideas of how you can integrate self-assessment into your practice:

- ✔ Make the self-assessments grade-free. Removing any attachment to grades promotes honesty on the part of the students and keeps the focus on learning and skill development – not on report card grades.
- ✔ Provide a rubric, checklist, or template for the students to complete, but leave space for open-ended comments. Students in grades 4 to 6 are not experts in defining different skills and understanding what separates different levels of proficiency. Providing a rubric, checklist, or some other type of template makes the self-assessment task easier, resulting in more students completing it. The students can use the content of the rubric to better understand how each skill is defined and what distinguishes higher levels or proficiency from lower levels.

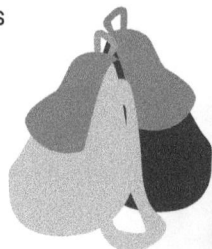

- Have a conversation with the student about their self-assessment. This conversation is critical if students are going to see this exercise as valuable. When self-assessments do not lead to conversations with the teacher (whether in-person or online) students see the self-assessment as a pointless exercise. You will be surprised by how much you learn about each student through these conversations!
- Link the self-assessment to goal setting and planning. The purpose of assessment is to improve student learning. Make this explicit by asking students to use their self-assessment to inform the development of learning goals and plans to achieve those goals. Note that goal setting and planning are important skills in their own right.

Example: Sample Digital Skills Self-Assessment

I share my password	With anyone	With friends	With close friends and family	With my parents only
I can tell when an email is suspicious	Rarely	Sometimes	Usually	Always
I return the computer or tablet and plug in the charger	Rarely	Sometimes	Usually	Always
I tell the teacher if a computer or tablet has a problem	Rarely	Sometimes	Usually	Always
I use the computer or tablet for learning purposes in the classroom	Rarely	Sometimes	Usually	Always
I access websites that are NOT allowed by the school	Rarely	Sometimes	Usually	Always
I can use keyboard shortcuts like CTRL-C, CTRL-V, and CTRL-Z	I don't know any shortcuts	I know one shortcut	I know 2 or 3 short cuts	I know 4 or more shortcuts
I let the teacher or my parents know when cyberbullying happens	Rarely	Sometimes	Usually	Always
I verify information I get from a website using a book, another website, or other resource	Rarely	Sometimes	Usually	Always
I share personal information about myself on the internet	Never	Rarely	Sometimes	Often
I check with my teacher or parent before downloading anything onto my computer	Never	Rarely	Sometimes	Often

Teacher Assessment

Rubrics are useful tools for both summative and formative assessment. Developing a rubric with colleagues allows different perspectives to inform the rubric and initiates a rich, professional discussion about skill development and assessment. These discussions can take place as part of a professional learning community, professional development day or workshop, or during school meetings.

The example rubric below is for collaboration. It is one possible rubric, but many other possibilities exist. What is important is that the rubric is sensible, usable, and there is consensus on implementing it.

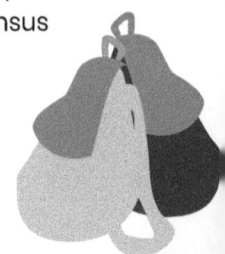

Example: Collaboration Rubric

	Not meeting expectations	Approaching expectations	Meeting expectations	Exceeding expectations
Contributions	Contributions are often negative, irrelevant, or distract the group from accomplishing its task.	Contributions are sometimes positive, and some help the group accomplish its task.	Contributions are positive and usually help the group accomplish its task.	Contributions are thoughtful, positive, and help the group accomplish its task. Encourages contributions from other group members
Attitude	Attitude is often negative and impedes other group members from wanting to participate.	Sometimes displays a positive attitude, but other times the attitude can be negative or problematic.	Usually displays a positive attitude.	Always displays a positive attitude, enhancing the confidence and willingness of other group members.
Listening	Rarely listens or pays attention to the contributions of others. Interrupts frequently.	Sometimes loses focus when listening to others or interrupts occasionally at inopportune times.	Listens well to other group members.	Listens actively and attentively to other group members.
Task performance	Work is not completed on time and/or the quality is low enough to impede accomplishing the task.	Work is completed to a reasonable standard and is done on time.	Work is completed to a good standard and is done on time.	Work is completed to a high standard, well organized, and is done on time or early.
Leadership	Absences from meetings meant the person often did not understand tasks and could not complete their obligations. Often distracted others or behaved in a manner that impeded the group's progress	Participated in most meetings. Completed their obligations.	Participated in all meetings. Completed their obligations and encouraged others where necessary.	Participated in all meetings. Completed their obligations while encouraging and assisting others where necessary. Recognized when the group needed direction or leadership and took action to keep the group productive.

Another possible assessment idea is illustrated below for questioning skills. We want students to develop the ability to ask relevant, insightful questions that are likely to lead to further learning. The chart links different sorts of questions to Bloom's taxonomy. Bloom's Taxonomy is familiar to many K–12 teachers. This makes it an attractive framework to use in assessing student questioning as teachers do not have to learn a new framework and are able to apply this one right away. The example questions are all related to science, but a similar chart could be made for any subject area. Such a chart could be used to give students feedback on the questions they ask, it could be used to help students self-assess their own questions, or it could be used to anchor assignments related to questioning.

Example: Using Bloom's Taxonomy to Assess Questioning Skills

Bloom's Level	Types of Questions	Example Questions
Remember	Factual Recall Questions	What are the three main types of rocks? Which type of rock is usually layered?
Understand	Comparison questions, explanations, inferences and classification questions	Why do metamorphic rocks often have alternating dark and light bands? Two fossils are found is sedimentary rock, but one fossil is found 3 meters deeper than another. Which fossil is likely to be older and why?
Apply	Questions about executing or implementing knowledge	How could one make educated theories about whether a mountain range was once underwater? How can I test which rocks contain iron?
Analyze	Questions about how different parts relate to each other, or create a whole system.	How is a rock's hardness related to its formation? What are some limiting factors in allowing us to recycle different minerals?
Evaluate	Questions about worth or criteria for assessing worth. Critiques.	What materials would be most suitable to use for paving roads? Consider cost, environmental impact, availability of the material, and ease of use. What are some weaknesses with using visual observation to determine type of rock? What are some other tests one can use and why are they better?
Create	How to make a new or novel product.	Design an experiment to determine which of these ten rocks is the hardest. Write a story about how a fossil is created. It must be written from the point of view of the animal or plant that was fossilized.

Key findings from our study

We have already described how both practicing and pre-service teachers see a range of skills as being important to develop in grades 4 to 6 students. When we asked educators what skills they spend the most time developing in their classroom there was a 4-way tie with literacy, numeracy, creativity, and responsibility. All four of these skills are career-related skills but as we noted earlier, they are career-related because

they are useful in almost all aspects of one's life. The skill that educators reported spending the least time on developing was digital skills. Our research did not uncover why this was the case, but we did note that digital skills were not seen as important by grade 4 to 6 educators and so it makes sense that little time would be spent developing them in those classrooms.

When our survey asked for appropriate ways for students to learn the skill the respondent ranked as most important, educators selected teacher-led instruction in the classroom most often. Surprisingly, unstructured play was selected second most often (tied with experiential or hands-on learning in the classroom) highlighting the value that teachers place upon unstructured play. The least often mentioned methods of learning were through outside lessons (e.g., piano lessons), sports, and one-on-one tutoring. Table 9 shows the prevalence of all responses to the item.

Table 9.

Educators' and parents' responses to the appropriate way for grade 4 to 6 children to learn key skills

Statement	Educator Prevalence	Parent Prevalence	Pre-Service Teacher Prevalence
In the classroom using teacher directed lessons	18%	11%	100%
Unstructured play	15%	11%	0%
In the classroom through experiential or hands-on learning	15%	18%	0%
Through field trips or experiences in places of work	13%	13%	0%
Extracurricular activities	10%	14%	0%
At home with the family	10%	15%	0%
Sports	7%	8%	0%
One on one tutoring	7%	3%	0%
Lessons outside of school	5%	8%	0%

Table 9 shows that elementary educators are aware of, and see value in, a wide range of learning methods. We found an interesting contrast with the responses of pre-service teachers. All pre-service teachers (100%) said that "In the classroom using teacher directed lessons" was the most appropriate way for grade 4 to 6 students to learn key skills. While our research did not uncover the reasons for this view among pre-service teachers, it would seem that as teachers gain experience, they become more aware of the different ways that children learn. It should be noted that parents held similar views to practicing educators in that they saw a range of methods and activities as being appropriate for grade 4 to 6 students to learn key skills although parents appeared to place greater value on experiential and hands-on learning than educators.

Example activities for you to think about

In the next section of this toolkit, you will find a small selection of activities that we hope will inspire you to bring to life some of the topics in this chapter in your teaching practice. Please feel free to adapt these activities to suit your individual learning environment.

Activity:
Matching Game

Aim: To have students consider the connection between different skills and where they may be useful in life.

Activity Description:

Set up: Students work in pairs and each pair needs a set of "Skills" cards. The teacher will have a set of "Experience" cards that are not visible to the students (see Appendix A and B for a printable template for both sets of cards).

Game Play: Once the students have their "Skills" cards and are ready to play, the teacher picks an "Experience" card at random and shows it to the students. Each pair of students then must come to a consensus about which 3 skills are most important for this experience. They students hold up their three cards so the teacher can see them. The teacher then asks some pairs to justify their choice of skills noting commonalities and differences among the groups. Note that it is this discussion that forms the core learning in this activity. By hearing different perspectives and rationales, the students can learn more about different skills and their importance in different contexts.

Example: The teacher holds up the "Babysitting" experience card. One pair of students holds up the "Problem solving", "Having empathy for other" and "Being responsible" skills cards. The teacher could ask that pair of students why they selected those three skills. If another pair selected different cards (e.g., "Reading", "Confidently speaking to others", and "Listening to others") the teacher could initiate and guide a discussion as to why different pairs selected different skills as being most important.

Career Connections:

The templates for the skills cards and experience cards have some blanks so teachers can include their own skills or experiences.

Teachers may want to briefly describe each experience to help students think about what skills might be important for that experience.

Activity:
Co-creating a Skills Rubric

Aim: To enhance students' understanding of a particular skill and clarify how that skill is assessed and developed in the classroom.

Activity Description: All Canadian public-school systems ask teachers to assess aspects of student performance beyond academic achievement. This portion of the report card has different labels such as *work habits*, *learning skills*, *cross-curricular competencies*, and *core competencies*. This is the section of the report card where teachers communicate about student performance in skills such as collaboration, responsibility, organization, and self-regulation. Often, students do not understand these terms and do not know how they are being assessed.

Co-creating rubrics with students can:

- lead to mutual understanding of the skill
- provide clarity about how the skill is assessed
- allow students to better understand the teacher's expectations
- provide guidance on how to provide feedback

Many teachers have experience co-constructing rubrics with students and so may have their own process. Here is one possible process for developing a rubric to assess collaboration. One could use this process for any skill or competency.

1. Begin with a general conversation about collaboration. What is it and why is it a useful skill? If students are not already familiar with rubrics, the concept of a rubric will need to be introduced.
2. Think pair share – what does it look like when someone is an excellent collaborator? What are the different components of collaboration? This step is used to generate words and ideas to be used in the next step.
3. In small groups (3 or 4 students) students will develop their own rubric. The teacher can provide some advice and guiding questions such as "What separates excellent collaboration from good collaboration?", "What feedback can we give others to help them improve their collaborative skills?", and "How could a student use this rubric to self-assess collaboration?"
4. Come together as a whole group and use the different rubrics and ideas presented to come to a consensus on the final rubric that will be used for the whole class.

Career Connections:

Consider how the rubric could be matched to the report cards. For instance, if the report cards use descriptors like "Excellent," "Good," "Satisfactory," and "Needs Improvement" you could use those descriptors in the rubric.

Different types of rubrics exist (e.g., analytic, single-point, holistic). Consider which type will work best for your students.

Having students self-assess their skills can lead to interesting and productive conversations about their learning.

Activity:
Show-Off Your skills!

Aim: To have students self-assess their areas of strength and to share that assessment with peers.

Activity Description: Students often have a strong sense of what skills they are good at and where they feel less confident. This activity asks students to share what skills they are good at. This is not only a chance for students to showcase their strengths but also a chance for the teacher to point out the diverse skills and abilities that exist within the classroom.

The activity follows the steps below:

1. Introduce the activity and give students 5 minutes to think about an ability they are good at. They can select any ability they want whether it is related to school or not (e.g., gymnastics, video games, imagination, math, reading, playing piano, etc.)
2. Students create a drawing that depicts the ability they are good at.
3. Students present their drawing to the class and explain what they are good at, how they got to be good, and why they think they are good.
4. As each student presents, the teacher writes on the board about the ability the student is good at. This is in preparation for a gallery walk, so there should be as much space as possible between the different abilities. If your classroom does not have a large space for writing, the teacher can write each ability on a separate sheet of paper and tape the paper to the wall or place it on the ground around the classroom.
5. The teacher leads a brief, whole class discussion about the diverse range of skills and abilities within the classroom and how different people contribute to their community in different ways.
6. Students pair up and each pair are given post-it notes on which to write a single foundational skill (e.g., adaptability, collaboration, problem-solving, math, reading, computer skills). You can create your own list of skills or use the list given in Appendix C.
7. Student pairs walk around the room and for each ability written by the teacher, the student pair selects a post-it note (skill) to place next to that ability. They should select a skill they think is needed to develop this ability.
8. Once the post-it notes are placed, the class regroups, and the teacher leads a whole class discussion about how different skills are applied in different areas of life. It can be interesting to note which skills applied to many different abilities and which were more specific.

Career Connections:

This activity is a great opportunity to acknowledge and celebrate the different abilities and skills that students bring to the class.

This activity provides a bridge between school and home life.

The different abilities could form the basis of a display highlighting the strengths of each student.

Evaluating the journey: How do I know this is worthwhile?

This chapter has already given multiple ideas and strategies for assessing students' skill development. With that in mind, we encourage you to consider the following questions to further refine your practice:

- How can I be more intentional in my practice when it comes to nurturing and developing children's fundamental skills?
- What skills are important for students to develop to be successful in school, life, and beyond? What transferable skills can I help students develop for a future that is yet to unfold?
- What skills are emphasized within the guiding curriculum and policy documents I work with on a daily basis?
- In what ways do I help to nurture and develop fundamental skills in my daily practice with students? To what extent do I provide students with a balance of structured and unstructured activities and endeavours to practice, develop, and refine fundamental skills?
- To what extent do my assessment practices support the goals of skill development? How might I further advance and refine these practices?

Journey reflections: Key takeaways

Foundational skills are synonymous with career-related skills, essential skills, and life skills. Developing these skills among children and youth is important as they not only underpin academic success but success in life as well.

Many different skills are useful in school, work, and everyday life. So, it can be difficult to identify what skills to focus on within the classroom and school. Trying to address too many skills at once will likely lead to challenges and an inability to explore and/or develop any skill effectively. Thus, teachers may find it rewarding to place emphasis on exploring and developing fewer skills in deep and meaningful ways.

Foundational skills are nurtured and developed at school through structured activities, such as lessons and planned experiences, and unstructured opportunities, such as free play and recess. Teachers can support career-related learning and skill development through intentional teaching, learning, and assessment practices that incorporate a variety of teacher- and student-directed experiences.

Chapter 4
It Takes a Village!
A Collaborative and Community-Based Approach

Exploring the possibilities: What is this chapter about?

This chapter introduces a variety of different groups and individuals in your local and broader communities who are potentially valuable contributors and partners in creating effective career-related learning for your students. Through this chapter you will be able to identify who these groups and individuals are and think about what their roles might be in supporting your classroom practices. Importantly, this chapter will help you to think about the advantages of and various ways to engage with members of your community to enhance the career-related learning experiences of your students.

This chapter acknowledges that while most career development activities are focused on the needs and outcomes for individuals, career-related learning does not take place in a vacuum. Young people interact with career-related learning everyday within a milieu consisting of peers, families and carers, and local, regional, national, and global communities. Subsequently, when developing quality career development activities, we can reach out to members of these communities as partners and co-contributors of new, innovative, and creative approaches to career-related learning and skill development. In embracing an inclusive approach, educators can help young people forge connections between the career-related knowledge and skills they are developing and their learning, lives, and future work environments in ways that are meaningfully connected to their communities and lived experiences.

Why should I be reading this chapter?

As you interact with this chapter, we aim to inspire you to think about the variety of ways that you and your school community can engage with your parents, carers, and broader community groups. A combined collaborative and community approach is not a one-way process! Schools are the heart of many communities, and many community groups and employers might have valuable resources to invest in their local schools. For example, employer engagement activities often provide great opportunities for staff development for employees of organizations with added benefits for your classroom (Stuart, 2014). Employers can also contribute innovative approaches to activities for your classroom that support students' skills development, enhancing a child's educational

experience. In addition, building relationships with community groups can create openings for class visits, partnerships, and for inviting Elders and other community leaders into your classroom. Such experiences create important occasions for relationship building and provide students pathways to new experiences and learning beyond the classroom.

This chapter embraces a focus toward thinking of a career-related learning environment as a *village* where schools and community partners develop collaborative and shared visions for helping students to become lifelong learners and informed citizens. This social practice theory toward careers learning (Thomsen, 2012) allows collaborators to come together to build effective and innovative learning environments where new approaches and opportunities for young people to engage in thinking about their future participation in education and society are created and sustained. This is an exciting approach rooted in community participation where schools play an active leadership role in creating and implementing a sustainable and optimized career-related learning and skills building agenda.

Planning and packing for the journey: What do I need to be thinking about?

Having set out a vision for a collaborative approach, we invite you to think about who your key *partners* and *communities* might be. To help you in this process, we offer some discussion about what we mean by these two terms.

Who are the partners?

For the purposes of this chapter, partners are individuals or organizations who have a vested interest in the outcomes of career development and are committed to its continuation. We can think of partners in two broad groups: internal partners (those individuals who work within or directly with a school) and external partners (everyone else) who have a shared interest. Each of these groups will be approaching career development from a different perspective and may have different skill sets and expertise to offer.

Internal partners (e.g., educators, administrators, or senior management) have a shared commitment to the students in their school in helping students aspire and achieve through the delivery of a high-quality educational experience. For these partners, understanding the potential of providing high-quality career-related learning activities and how they can positively impact the overall mission and goals of the school is crucial. In Chapter Three, we demonstrated the role of career-related learning in developing life and foundational skills, such as critical thinking, communication, and teamwork.

External partners often bring different perspectives and experiences than internal partners. For example, some businesses may have corporate social responsibility targets and can fulfill these by working with schools. In some cases, this contribution provides support for the attainment of equipment, trips, or other resources or to fund competitions or enterprise activities. More likely, it is through providing resources to support formal and informal career-related learning, such as mentoring, in-school visits (e.g., guest speaker, special assembly), or input into some lessons or activities.

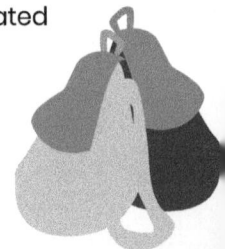

Volunteer organizations are also potential partners. Youth and community groups may understand the important and positive impact that high quality career related learning can have on positive mental health, creating a sense of belonging, and introducing notions of peace and justice. Organizations such as the Lions Club have a strong commitment to support education and to grow local economies. A further example is how the providers of the Duke of Edinburgh Award for Canadian Youth work through a range of organizations including schools to engage young people in positive activities, which contribute to their personal, career, and employability development. There are many other provincial/territorial and federal groups who interact with and provide services for young people, and we encourage you to familiarize yourself with those in your locale to explore possibilities for productive career-related learning partnerships.

Some potential partners may not seem to be obvious choices for connecting with to build your career-related learning work, and thinking creatively about who and what is available in your community can help you to see new possibilities. For example, members of special interest areas, such as local sport teams or clubs, art-based organizations (e.g., dance or theatre companies), coaches, or music teachers, are valuable potential partners. Consider the opportunities that engaging in a local music or theatre production could have on young people's understanding of potential future career pathways as well as in developing excellent skills for life!

You might think about partnering with your local Indigenous community for some of your initiatives. It is important to consider how Indigenous peoples have been impacted by the disruptive legacy of colonialism and be mindful of how externally imposed power dynamics have disturbed and harmed so many Indigenous communities. Subsequently, it is crucial to not overburden your local communities, and be respectful and authentic as you reach out to begin forging relationships with them. Be willing to listen and learn, not make assumptions, and build your knowledge and understanding. Your career-related learning activities will be much richer and more valuable for all your learners as a result.

Parents and caregivers can also be considered partners. They have a vested interest in their child's success both in the classroom and beyond. Many are also employers or employees and might be able to support the school through this aspect of their working lives. Beyond sharing insights about their working lives, parents and caregivers can also share unique and lived experiences. Some parents might be time-rich and will be able to support through volunteering their time, mentoring, or providing support for visits or informal curriculum activities.

The National Career Development Association (NCDA; 2011) suggest that parents and caregivers and teachers can work together to develop many useful personal and career-related, skills such as collaboration, problem solving, creative thinking, and following directions as these are useful both at school and at home. Research in the UK, found that many parents feel underconfident in supporting their children with career decision making (Barnes et al., 2020). This finding is especially concerning given that parents are the biggest influence on children's career decision-making (Let's Talk Science, 2014). The NCDA (2011) noted the importance of supporting parents to understand the relationship between school subjects and future career choice. Parents can also play a key role in helping students to understand the role of work and its contribution to communities and society.

As you think more deeply about your local and broader community, an important aspect of being successful in engaging with external partners is to understand their motivations and identify possible benefits for them in helping you with career-related activity in your classroom and school.

Let's pause our journey...

Who are the internal and external partners and stakeholder groups that you might want to engage with?

What are their motivators for being involved in the school and for supporting good career development practices?

What do we mean by communities?

A community comprises individuals who have a particular characteristic in common. One traditional view of community is that they exist, live, or work in proximity. However, the internet has removed the notion of geographic location when defining community. There are different ways of categorizing communities. Thomsen (2017) suggests that community is:

- characterized by people conducting their daily lives (or parts of them) together in the same physical or virtual place;
- sustained and created through individuals' joint actions; and
- comprised of people who have different reasons for being there and for taking part in different ways which are changing over time. (p. 1)

Millington (2010) suggests that there are five types of community:

- **Interest:** Communities of people who share the same interest or passion.
- **Action:** Communities of people trying to bring about change.
- **Place:** Communities of people brought together by geographic boundaries.
- **Practice:** Communities of people in the same profession or undertake the same activities.
- **Circumstance:** Communities of people brought together by external events/ situations.

So, how do these definitions inform our approach to career development in elementary school? The first task for anyone wishing to begin a more collaborative approach is to understand that they will be engaging with more than one community. Some examples might include local Indigenous communities or Deaf community. There may also be community groups focused on sustainability or environmental impact. There will also be communities of individuals who are focused on developing and delivering good quality career development practices (e.g., local or regional professional associations). There may be differences in the way remote communities engage in the online space compared to those in urban or rural settings. Each of these groups may have a vested interest in supporting your school to develop and implement good career development practices.

Making the case for collaborative approaches

Undertaking collaborative activity is not without challenges. It can be time consuming and require some new knowledge or skills to pursue these approaches. It may not be immediately obvious that this type of approach can enhance existing pedagogical activities and it is likely that you will need to persuade senior leaders of the efficacy of this type of activity. You will, therefore, need to think about and prepare a strong rationale for undertaking this type of activity. You might want to consider:

- How is the school already engaging with partners and communities? Does the school have a policy or procedures in place for this type of work? Is there a named person with this area of responsibility in the school?
- What are the industries and employers who are operating locally? Are any of these new to the area? What is the mix of small-, medium-, and large-scale employers in the area?
- What is the rate of employment like in the area? Is there a lot of adult unemployment in the area? What about the rate of employment among the parents in your school?

Key findings from our study

In our study, we sought input from parents and business/industry partners regarding their involvement in career-related learning.

Support for career-related learning from parents

Parents value career related learning by examining their involvement with such learning (Table 10). Parents agreed that the skills needed to do well at school are similar to the ones needed for success in adulthood and also gave their child(ren) strategies to develop such skills. There was further evidence that parents talk to their child(ren) about jobs and careers and that parents value the foundational skills that underpin scholastic and career success.

Table 10.

Percentage of parents who agreed with statements related to their involvement with career-related learning

Statement	Percentage who agreed
I know what jobs my child has considered for their future	75%
I link the schoolwork my child completes with potential careers	31%
My child's report card contains comments about important skills such as collaboration, organization, and self-regulation.	93%
At parent-teacher interviews, my child's teacher talks to me about my child's transferable skills such as time management, communication, and conflict resolution.	62%
I give my child strategies to help them remember to complete their obligations such as cleaning their room or homework.	90%
The skills needed to do well at school are similar to those needed to do well in adulthood.	90%
My child tells me about interesting jobs or careers they have learned about at school	28%
Grade 5 children should be thinking about their future careers	62%
Elementary teachers play a vital role in developing career related skills	86%
A summer job working at McDonald's is a part of someone's career	83%

Support for career-related learning from business and industry partners

We also sought input from business and industry partners, arguably an important potential community partner for all elementary schools. Though we had a limited range of responses, respondents to the business industry survey were supportive of career education for students in grades 4 to 6 and saw elementary schools and teachers as having a role to play in the development of foundational skills and influencing career pathways.

Table 11.

Percentage of parents who agreed with statements relating to career education

Statement	Percentage who agreed
It is appropriate for Grade 5 students to be thinking about their future career path	80%
Elementary teachers play a vital role in developing career related skills	80%
Elementary schooling has a big influence on students' career choices	60%
Career education should be explicitly included somewhere in the curriculum in Grades 4 to 6.	80%
A summer job at McDonald's is part of someone's career	67%

All respondents believed career-related learning should start in elementary school with 40% saying it should start in grades 4 to 6 and another 40% saying it should start in grades 2 or 3. All respondents (100%) also said that members of the business community should have some responsibility for educating grade 4 to 6 children about careers, which contrasted with the parent and educator results. Business/Industry survey respondents also indicated that parents and teachers have an important role to play.

When asked what aspects of a job are most important, the views of the business/industry respondents were almost identical to those of parents. Being happy was viewed as most important with taking a job that meets the expectations of the family being least important (see Figure 1).

Figure 1.

Business/Industry respondents' view of the importance of different aspects of jobs.

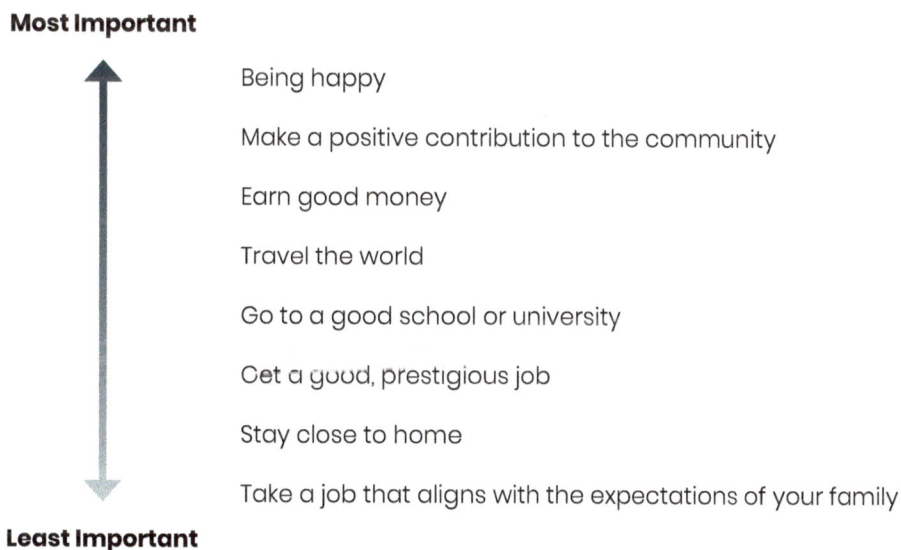

Most Important

Being happy

Make a positive contribution to the community

Earn good money

Travel the world

Go to a good school or university

Get a good, prestigious job

Stay close to home

Take a job that aligns with the expectations of your family

Least Important

Experiencing the journey: How does this chapter come to life in my classroom?

As we have seen, your school may be the centre of a rich source of support for career development work. With some careful thought and planning, you can leverage this resource to enhance the educational experience of your students and help position your school at the centre of a new approach to community collaboration. This section will explore practical ways of engaging these individuals and groups and highlight the necessity of scanning the landscape, creating a vision, checking your target groups have the experience and skills that they need, developing a program of support, and identifying any curriculum opportunities for integrating career-related learning.

Scanning the landscape

When embracing a collaborative and community-based approach, you may want to begin by imagining and exploring the possibilities. A good place to start is to undertake a short piece of research about potential partners and community members and how they might contribute to your initiative. This activity will help you to clearly articulate your vision and begin to better understand the potential for and scope of your project. For example, you may want to record this information using a mapping document (see Figure 2).

Figure 2.
Scanning the landscape activity

Stakeholder or community	Contact details or means of communicating or Web address	How might this group contribute?	Action/outcome

Creating a vision

Engaging with partners and communities can be time consuming. However, the rewards can be invaluable! Your first step should be to carefully think through a strong rationale for undertaking this work and to present it in a short document that can be shared with your leadership team and relevant staff. Your vision document should include:

- An inspirational statement about the potential for collaborative working
- A statement of purpose (what you hope to achieve by this initiative)
- A brief overview of the partners and communities that you wish to involve
- When you hope to undertake these activities
- How you will evaluate the impact of this initiative

Of course, you are more likely to have success if you have consulted with your colleagues about this endeavour before preparing your vision document.

Checking your target groups have the experience and skills that they need

To maximize the impact of any collaborative activity, it is important to recognize that not every willing volunteer has the necessary experience or skills to deliver effective educational interventions. Pan European research showed that not all parents feel confident to have career-related discussions with their child (Moore et al., 2021). This finding raises the question of what knowledge, skills, and attributes parents and caregivers need to support their child and whose responsibility it is to help them develop foundational skills, knowledge, and understanding. Moore et al. generated a framework of learning outcomes for parents that schools can use to reflect on this type of collaborative activity. This framework includes a section for parents of elementary schools. Highlighted are some important constructs that parents should know:

- The difference between, job, work, and skills.
- Fanciful ideas are ok realism comes later.
- People in the family and community are important role models for future success.
- There should not be pressure to choose 'a career'. Believing that you have a choice is more important.

In addition, parents should be encouraged to:

- Talk about how people work and the value and contribution that work makes to family and the community.
- Encourage their children to think positively about their future and the roles they would like to fulfil.
- Encourage their children to think about a broad range of jobs even if they seem fanciful or unrealistic.
- Celebrate the achievements of all the members of the family however unimportant or irrelevant they may seem.
- Reinforce the relationship between effort and reward. This does not have to be linked to extrinsic rewards (e.g., money) but can be about intrinsic rewards such as feelings of well-being or gaining new knowledge, skills, or confidence through experiences.

In terms of personal attributes, it is desirable for parents to:

- Be positive role models.
- Encourage a love of learning.
- Be aspirational.
- Be open and willing to talk about work.
- Be community minded.
- Value their own achievements. (Moore et al., 2021, p. 65)

You will also need to think about the learning needs of your students and consider if they have the skills and relevant prior knowledge needed to make sense of and engage with the career-related issues which are being introduced to them.

Let's pause our journey...

How can you use this framework for parents to develop support systems?

Could this framework wholly or in part relate to other partners and community members that you want to engage with?

Developing a program of support

Once you have identified any knowledge or skills gaps, you can consider how you will address these areas. There are many ways of communicating your vision and opportunities to partners and communities such as through your school's website (e.g., set up a page that explains your vision for career-related learning and life skill development in your classroom). Think about ways to communicate with any internal and external partners (e.g., you could use fact sheets or infographics to display in your classroom). Staff and parent meetings are also a great time to communicate your ideas and for reaching out to volunteers.

Identifying curriculum opportunities

There are many fun and informative activities that you can do with younger students to help them to connect their learning to their thinking about their future selves. Some of these activities may already be embedded into formal curriculum, such as having a guest speaker visit to talk about their work linked to a particular curriculum subject. Some examples might be:

- Medical practitioners talking about how their job involves elements of science and math.
- Artists and performers linking the skills they use in their work to key skills such as communication and teamwork.
- Construction workers talking about the use of mathematics and planning in their work.

Many schools already take students out of school on visits to a variety of events and spaces in their local communities. We encourage you to think about ways that such visits can be adapted to include career-related learning outcomes (e.g., by asking those hosting the visit to talk about their roles or the day-to-day work and activities that they perform).

Example activities for you to think about

In the next section of this toolkit, you will find a small selection of activities that we hope will inspire you to bring to life some of the topics in this chapter in your teaching practice. Please feel free to adapt these activities to suit your individual learning environment.

Activity: Community Café

Aim: Involve parents and the community in supporting career related learning

Activity Description: The teacher invites parents, family members, or community members to the class to talk about their own, jobs, careers, and life experiences. There are several possible to structure this. Some examples include:

- Have a community day and invite multiple parents and community members to speak and interact with the class (e.g., a panel, or a set of stations that students can visit).
- Make it a monthly event where a parent or community member speaks to the class
- Host an "Lunch and Learn" where students and community members interact.

Consider a broad range of parents and community members to invite. This could include:

- Retired people
- Volunteers
- Community advocates
- People in a broad range of jobs and industries
- Stay at home parents
- People from different cultural backgrounds (e.g., Indigenous, newcomers to Canada, rural, urban)

These types of events can be formal or informal depending on what you feel would work best for your students and community members.

Career Connections:

It can sometimes be challenging to get people to come during school hours. Consider inviting people from within the school community, using school newsletters and parent emails to recruit participants, and coordinating with community organizations. Think about how you might use outdoor or non-traditional learning spaces for this activity. Consider how you extend gratitude to the parents/community members.

Activity: Doing Something Big

Aim: Students will work in groups to envision all the people that would be needed to accomplish a big task. Because this activity identifies many different jobs and roles within the community, it is a useful starting point for learning about specific jobs.

Activity Description: Students will work in small groups (2 to 3) to identify a big, meaningful project and all the people that would need to be involved. This activity comprises multiple steps.

1. As a whole class, brainstorm some ideas for big projects. Examples might include opening a restaurant, building a playground, starting a charity, improving the city recycling program, cleaning up a local river, shooting a movie, creating a video game. There are LOTS of potential ideas.
2. Students are organized into groups of 2 or 3 based upon their interest in a particular project.
3. Students brainstorm all the different people and positions needed for their big project. The teacher will need to circulate and offer some suggestions to spur their thinking. For instance, opening a restaurant may require financing and grade 4 to 6 students are unlikely to think of this.
4. Students are given choice in how to record their thinking. Chart paper, Google Sheets, Lists, and other communication tools could be used.
5. Students present their findings to the whole class. The whole class can ask questions and offer input to help groups refine their work further.

Career Connections:

The activity could be adapted so the entire class focuses on one large project. Small groups generate ideas independently and then come together to share ideas and create a whole class vision of who should be involved in the project.

This activity could be tied to Community Café depending on the expertise of community members

Activity:
Talks from people about their jobs

Aim: To help students learn more about jobs and occupations and provide a realistic picture of what happens in different occupations, and what some people in their local communities and businesses do in regard jobs and work-related activities.

Activity Description:

1. Invite a range of guest speakers to come and visit your school to discuss a range of work occupations and experiences.
2. Structure the time so that students have the chance to listen and ask questions.
3. Provide students with the opportunity to reflect on the session, consider adding a follow-up writing or presentation activity where they share what they have learned.

Many schools already have individuals in to talk about road safety, health etc. It is a small step to get these individuals to talk about their jobs.

Career Connections:

The activity could be adapted so the entire class focuses on one guest speaker and the class undertakes a group follow up project. This could take the form of a research assignment where students investigate more about the guest speaker and their organization, for example looking up the organizational mission and vision statement, who else works in the organization and what different job roles they have.

Activity:
Mini enterprise activity

Aim: Can help students participate in project-based learning where they are able to learn more about their local community

Activity Description:

1. Help students to brainstorm some ideas of how they could undertake a community action project. They should decide who they want to help, how they are going to plan and undertake their project.
2. Invite a community group or organization to partner with the students in some way. This might be a very hands-on involvement, or it might be a commitment to come and listen to the students as they present their project.
3. Provide students with a time frame, and time in class to undertake their project.
4. Ensure students understand what resources they do or do not have available to them.
5. Once students have decided on the issue, support their investigation to learn more and make an action plan.
6. At this point students carry out their plan. For example, if students have decided to start a supplies drive for a local animal shelter, it is their responsibility to get fliers or social media posts out there. You may need to offer guidance as to how the supplies will be delivered to the shelter, and this is where involving the shelter might be beneficial as they may be able to collect the supplies form the students whilst they are in school.
7. Advise students on how to evaluate their enterprise activity and arrange an opportunity for them to thank the community partner.

Career Connections:

Local employers or community partners may be willing to get involved in these and provide real case study activities for young people to work on. In addition, where charity or fundraising drives are taking place, these are great opportunities to get students to get involved in the planning, creating products for sale (cakes, crafts etc.) and to understand the commercial transactions and money handling skills required for success. These are all career and life skill development. With a little imagination, students can be helped to understand the relevance for their future lives.

Activity:
Scavenger Hunt

Aim: Students will explore the school community to learn more about the people and connections that make a school function.

Activity Description: This activity is a field trip around the school. Students will go with the teacher to different parts of the school to meet with members of the school community to learn about what they do and how they contribute to the functioning of the school. Before running this activity, we recommend consulting with your colleagues and administration so they can prepare for your class visit. Some possible members of the school community to visit would be:

- Other teachers and students
- Special education specialists
- Administrators
- Custodial staff
- Librarians
- Indigenous education specialists
- Lunch and playground supervisors
- Parent and community volunteers
- Educational assistants
- Student teachers
- IT staff
- Secretarial staff
- Crossing guards
- Bus drivers

Of course, this is not an exhaustive list, and you likely have other interesting members of your school community that your students would love to meet.

This activity could be connected to other teaching activities. Some suggestions are:

1. Have students work in pairs to interview a member of the school community and present their findings to the class.
2. Have students create a mind map about the school community before the field trip and then have them revisit and expand their mind maps after the field trip.
3. As a class, create a mural that illustrates the connectedness of the school community.

Career Connections:

This activity could be adapted to fit other contexts (e.g., community centres).

The field trip could happen in the local neighbourhood exposing the students to the broader community and the different people and positions that make up the community.

Evaluating the journey: How do I know this is worthwhile?

Persuading your colleagues to get involved in engaging partners and community members in career-related learning for elementary students may be a challenge. While there is some evidence that this approach can be very effective, you will need to provide evidence that this initiative is having the impact that you hoped it would. There are several steps in helping to understand the impact of an initiative. One theorist who set out a model for evaluation was Kirkpatrick (1967). His model shows that there can be different impacts of an activity, but these can take place at different stages after an event. A student's reaction can be measured immediately afterwards through a feedback sheet or discussion about how they feel. A little further after the event, it might be possible to measure their learning. This approach, of course, requires some clearly defined learning outcomes—but, there may be unintentional learning which may take place as well! A change in behaviour may be observed further from the event. For example, are children more engaged in their lessons as a result of an employer-led activity? Finally, it might be possible to determine the extent to which the school and staff have been impacted by the initiative. This impact may well be a longer-term evaluation and might include reflections on improved community relations, investment into the school through additional resources of both time and material goods. Figure 3 sets out Kirkpatrick's (1967) model.

Figure 3
Kirkpatrick's Model of Evaluation (1967)

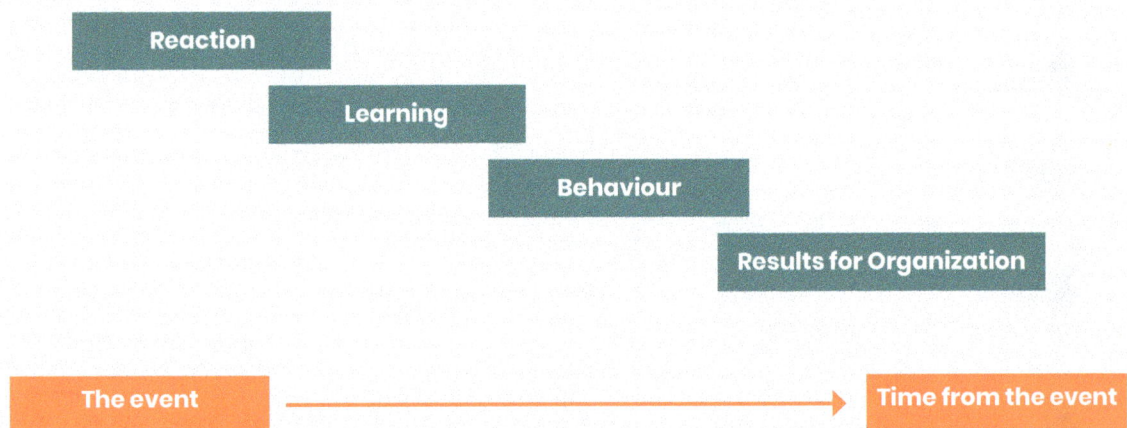

Let's pause our journey...

What approaches will you use to determine the different impacts of your activity?

How will you report the outcome of your reflections?

Journey reflections: Key takeaways from this chapter

It really does take a village to effectively support your students in their career-related learning! This approach brings complexities in navigating your local and broader community and engaging with the right people. However, the bonus is that you do not have to do this work alone.

Parents and carers are a really important source for you to tap into. They have a vested interest in the success of what happens in school as it directly affects their children.

Not all parents and carers are confident in what they are able to contribute, and it is important to find some small ways to make them feel valued. Equally this may open up opportunities for you to undertake career-related learning information sessions with your parents!

You can engage with folks in your school and outside of your school. Everyone has the potential to contribute and share something valuable. Think laterally as you seek such partners.

Engaging with others brings fresh perspectives and opportunities for rich learning for your students. These are essential in career-related learning and can be useful in other subject areas too.

Chapter 5
Curriculum Support for Career-Related Learning

Exploring the Possibilities: What is this chapter about?

This chapter provides an overview of how career-related learning appears in a variety of curriculum documents across different provinces and territories in Canada. Broadly, the approach to including career-related learning in the curriculum falls into three strands. Some provinces and territories, such as British Columbia, Ontario, New Brunswick, and Yukon, have embraced a kindergarten to grade 12 (K–12) approach to career education. In other areas of the country, career education begins to emerge in grades 5 and 6 (e.g., Alberta, Saskatchewan, and some of the Atlantic provinces). Still other regions do not appear to have any formal career education curricula currently in place at the elementary level (e.g., Nunavut). In some provinces and territories, there are specific career development and career-related policy and/or curriculum documents. However, in other jurisdictions career-related learning also appears in subject specific policy and curriculum documents.

Why should I be reading this chapter?

As an educator, you likely know the curriculum for core subject areas quite well. However, you might not know about specific career-related learning curriculum and policy, especially if thinking about career-related learning is new to you. Equally, because career-related learning can be embedded into other subject areas, or even when taught discretely, elements of career-related learning overlap with other subject areas. It is, therefore, a useful activity to (re)examine career-related curriculum and policy to both re-enforce knowledge and gain fresh insights.

In this chapter, we introduce some of the curriculum and policy documents that we feel are particularly relevant, informative, and interesting. Importantly, this sample illustrates how this toolkit aligns to many intended learning outcomes seen in career-related curricula from across Canada. To help you understand the range of approaches to career-related learning across Canada, we have focused on selected provinces and territories, and have presented these in three groups:

- Those with formal K–12 policy and curriculum;
- Those with a focus on grades 5–6 upwards; and
- Those without any formal career-related learning curriculum and where career-related learning is embedded into other curricula and subject areas.

We do not intend this chapter to be exhaustive—included here is just a taste of what is out there to support your practice. We encourage you to also explore the curriculum and policy documents specific to your jurisdiction to find further useful sources and resources that will support your career-related learning practice and activity.

Planning and packing for the journey: What do I need to be thinking about?

We begin our exploration of curriculum and policy documents with a focus on British Columbia and Ontario, both provinces having a formal K–12 policy and curriculum for career education. In each of the sections, we focus on jurisdictions in alphabetical order.

British Columbia

The curriculum for career education in British Columbia (BC) aims to offer learners "opportunities to explore and develop personal interests, strengths, and competencies while making connections with experiential learning, career-life possibilities, and preferred post-graduation opportunities" (British Columbia Ministry of Education, n.d.).

One useful aspect of the BC curriculum is its focus on career-life connections. The learning standards are split into two strands of curricula competency (what students are expected to be able to do) and content (what students are expected to know). Both strands point to worthwhile practices for career development including personal career-life development, connections with community, and career-life planning. The career-life connections Big Ideas can be seen in Figure 4.

Figure 4.
Big Ideas of Career-Life Connections

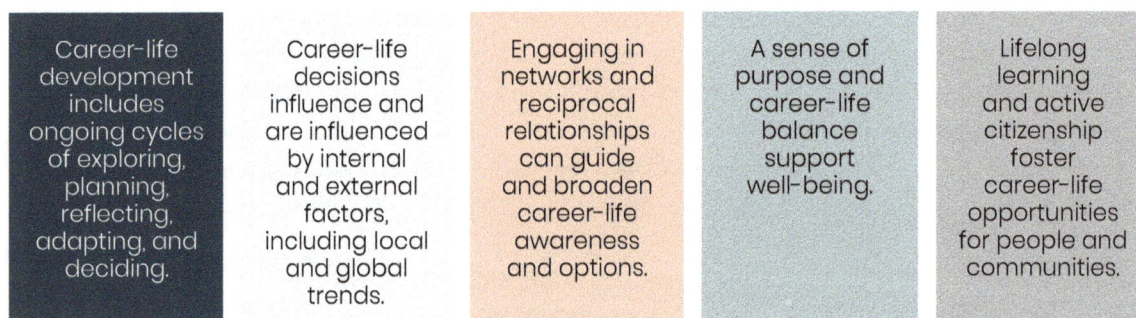

Career-life development includes ongoing cycles of exploring, planning, reflecting, adapting, and deciding.	Career-life decisions influence and are influenced by internal and external factors, including local and global trends.	Engaging in networks and reciprocal relationships can guide and broaden career-life awareness and options.	A sense of purpose and career-life balance support well-being.	Lifelong learning and active citizenship foster career-life opportunities for people and communities.

The BC curriculum website outlines the expectations and learning standards (curricula competency and content) for each grade, and identifies three core competencies of communication, thinking, and personal and social (see Table 12 for a sample of what this looks like for grade 4).

Table 12.

Career Education 4 [Grade 4] Core Competencies

Communication	Thinking	Personal and Social
Communicating	Critical and reflective thinking	Personal awareness and responsibility
Collaborating	Creative thinking	Positive personal and cultural identify
		Social awareness and responsibility

Each page for each grade also features Big Ideas. See Figure 5 for a sample of Big Ideas for grade 4.

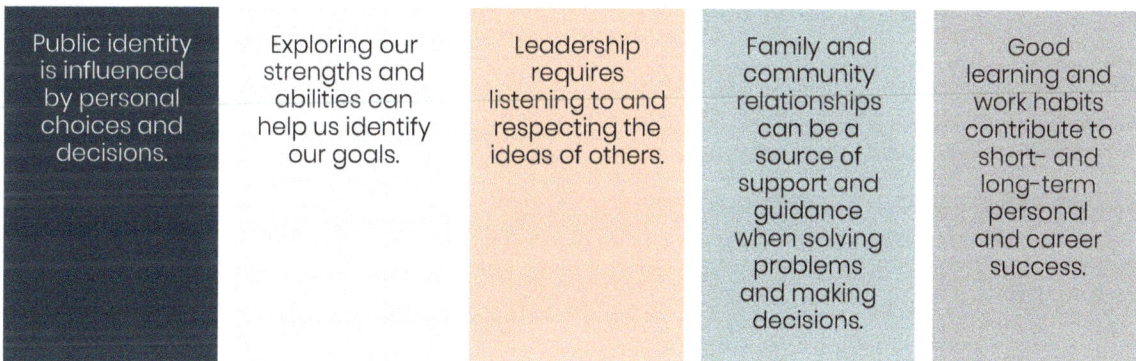

Figure 5.

Big Ideas for Grade 4

Public identity is influenced by personal choices and decisions.	Exploring our strengths and abilities can help us identify our goals.	Leadership requires listening to and respecting the ideas of others.	Family and community relationships can be a source of support and guidance when solving problems and making decisions.	Good learning and work habits contribute to short- and long-term personal and career success.

How can the BC curriculum help me?

The language and design of the BC career education curriculum provides a flexible approach for educators who wish to undertake career-related learning with their learners. There is lots of room within this curriculum for approaches to accommodate a range of learner interest, needs, goals, and the diversity of school and community contexts. Even if you are not located in BC, there are career-related ideas and practices that could easily be migrated to any jurisdiction and context. Notably, the emphasis on learners' personal career-life development, forging connections with community, and attention to career-life planning aligns with the focus of this toolkit.

> *"Practising respectful, ethical, inclusive behaviour prepares us for the expectations of the workplace...Safe environments depend on everyone following safety rules... New experiences, both within and outside of school, expand our career skill set and options."* (Government of British Columbia, n.d.)

Helpful Links: British Columbia

The British Columbia career education curriculum website can be found at https://curriculum.gov.bc.ca/curriculum/career-education

The focus on career-life connections can be found at https://curriculum.gov.bc.ca/curriculum/career-education/all/career-life-connections

For a more comprehensive overview of the British Columbia career education curriculum please refer to our literature review (2022) which can be found at https://ceric.ca/projects/career-development-in-children-identifying-critical-success-conditions-and-strategies/

Ontario

Creating Pathways to Success: An Education and Career/Life Planning Program for Ontario Schools was introduced by the Government of Ontario Ministry of Education in 2013. The goals of the education and career/life planning program are stated as (Government of Ontario, 2013):

- ensure that students develop the knowledge and skills they need to make informed education and career/life choices through the effective application of a four-step inquiry process;
- provide opportunities for this learning both in and outside the classroom; and
- engage parents and the broader community in the development, implementation, and evaluation of the program, to support students in their learning.

For these goals to be achieved, every elementary and secondary school is expected to develop, document, implement, and evaluate an education and career/life planning program based on the policies outlined in this document.

Creating Pathways to Success is an inquiry-based conceptual framework that guides schools in developing a comprehensive K–12 education and career/life planning program. The four-step inquiry process is built on four questions linked to the four areas of learning in education and career/life planning: Knowing Yourself; Exploring Opportunities; Making Decisions and Setting Goals; and Achieving Goals and Making Transitions (see Figure 6).

Figure 6.

The Four-Step Inquiry Process of the Education and Career/Life Planning Program

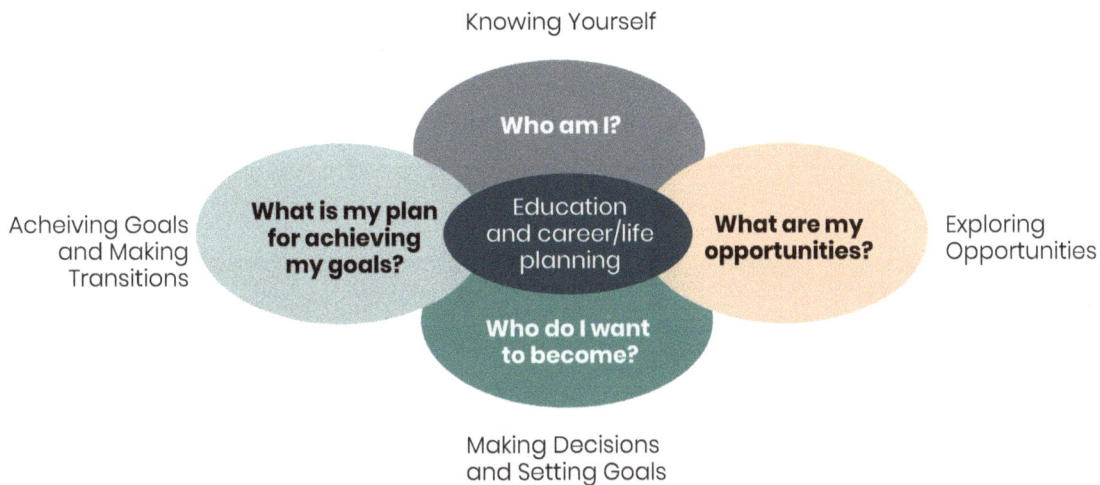

Knowing Yourself

Who am I?

Acheiving Goals and Making Transitions

What is my plan for achieving my goals?

Education and career/life planning

What are my opportunities?

Exploring Opportunities

Who do I want to become?

Making Decisions and Setting Goals

How can the Ontario curriculum help me?

The framework provides flexibility due to the emphasis that may be placed on different areas of learning at different stages of development and the activities involved. For example, in grades 4–6 when learners are actively learning about themselves and are exploring their worlds, the question *Who am I?* offers a natural point of entry into career-related learning. The framework highlights to educators how they can "encourage young students to become conscious of what they most love to do, what they do best, and how they feel when they are engaged in various activities" (Government of Ontario, 2013, p. 13). Teachers are encouraged to pose questions and guide students towards opportunities for exploring their passions and talents further, taking them into the second area of learning in the framework *Exploring Opportunities*.

> *"Teachers can encourage young students to become conscious of what they most love to do, what they do best, and how they feel when they are engaged in various activities. Teachers can pose questions and guide students towards opportunities for exploring their passions and talents further, taking them into the second area of learning in the framework – Exploring Opportunities."* (Government of Ontario, 2013, p. 13)

The value of engaging learners in the early grades in a variety of opportunities to reflect, develop self-knowledge, and build capacity to effectively plan is highlighted, making this curriculum a worthwhile read for any educator seeking to develop career-related learning in their school or district. The goals and aims of this curriculum align to the career-related learning approaches of this toolkit.

Helpful Links: Ontario

The Creating Pathways to Success: An Education and Career/Life Planning Program for Ontario Schools document can be found at **https://www.edu.gov.on.ca/eng/document/policy/cps/creatingpathwayssuccess.pdf**

Let's pause our journey...

Like BC and Ontario, do you have a K–12 type of curriculum approach in your own province or territory?

If so, how does this curriculum support your career-related learning?

If not, what might you be able to take away from the BC and/or Ontario career education curriculum to help you in your own jurisdiction?

We continue our exploration of curriculum and policy documents with a focus on Alberta and Saskatchewan, both provinces having policy and curriculum for career education in grades 5 and 6. Once again, we focus on jurisdictions in alphabetical order.

Alberta

In Alberta, the Career and Technology Foundations (CTF) is an optional program where learners can explore their interests and passions as they learn about various career possibilities and occupational areas (Alberta Education, 2017). The CTF Program of Studies is based on 14 learning outcomes that identify what students are expected to learn and what will be assessed. All 14 outcomes are the same for grades 5 to 9 (see Table 13). This curriculum intends to support programming decisions at the local level (e.g., time, resources, instructional approaches, assessment, reporting and organization for instruction), making CTF courses responsive to the needs of learners, teachers, schools, and communities.

Table 13.

Career and Technology Foundations (CTF) Learning Outcomes

CTF is exploring interests, passions and skills while making personal connections to career possibilities
- I explore my interests and passions while making personal connections to career possibilities
- I use occupational area skills, knowledge and technologies
- I follow safety requirements associated with occupational areas and related technologies
- I demonstrate environmental stewardship associated with occupational areas

CTF is planning, creating, appraising and communicating in response to challenges
- I plan in response to challenges
- I make decisions in response to challenges
- I adapt to change and unexpected events
- I solve problems in rewsponse to challenges
- I create products, performances or services in response to challenges
- I appraise the skills, knowledge and technologies used to respond to challenges
- I communicate my learning

CTF is working independently and with others while exploring careers and technology
- I determine how my actions affect learning
- I develop skills that support effective relationships
- I collaborate to achieve common goals

Career education in Alberta is also connected to *Cross-Curricular Competencies*, a set of attitudes, skills, and knowledge developed by every learner, in every grade, and across every subject/discipline area. These competencies are:

- identify and apply career and life skills
- know how to learn
- think critically
- identify and solve complex problems
- manage information
- innovate
- create opportunities
- apply multiple literacies
- demonstrate global and cultural understanding, and
- demonstrate good communication skills and the ability to work cooperatively with others. (Ministerial Order #001/2013)

Importantly, this range of skills aligns to many found in the Government of Canada's Skills for Success Framework (see Chapter Three: Nurturing and Developing Foundational Skills).

How can the Alberta curriculum help me?

The approach to introducing career-related learning in Alberta's schools reinforces the need to be flexible and adaptable to suit localized needs. This method is an important and foundational component for effective practice when career-related learning is aimed at equitably meeting the needs of a diverse range of students. A closer examination of the Alberta curriculum can help you to see how career-related learning can be found in many different areas of curriculum (e.g., health and life skills), providing you with a broad range of guidance documents to support your practice in your own jurisdiction.

Saskatchewan

Career Education in Saskatchewan aims to enable "students to develop essential skills and career management competencies to assist them in achieving their potential as they construct their personal life and work career" (Government of Saskatchewan, 2008, p. 4). Three overarching Career Education goals are identified as:

- all students will develop career management competencies through an exploration of personal change and growth;
- all students will explore the connections between learning and work pathways and their connections to community; and
- all students will engage in inquiry to construct a personal life and work plan.

These goals "identify a three-part plan of career development where students develop personal management to utilize career information while creating their career pathway" (p. 6). The Blueprint for Life/Work Designs (National Life/Work Centre) has been adopted as the "scope and sequence for the integration of career development competencies into all curricula" (p. 5), with the identified career development competencies forming the basis of the career education curriculum. Saskatchewan also draws on the Government of Canada's Essential Skills Framework.

How can the Saskatchewan curriculum help me?

The Saskatchewan curriculum includes a detailed section on teaching career education in schools and assessment and evaluation of learning. Many of the principles outlined support the approaches we recommend in this toolkit. Of particular interest is a section on how to create questions for inquiry in career education and how to make connections with students' lives, previous learning, and learning in other subject areas (see Figure 7). This information helps highlight the value of career-related learning as an adaptable curriculum that can support across-school teaching and learning (Government of Saskatchewan, 2008, pp. 6–17).

Figure 7.

Career Education Grade 6, Connections with Other Areas of Study

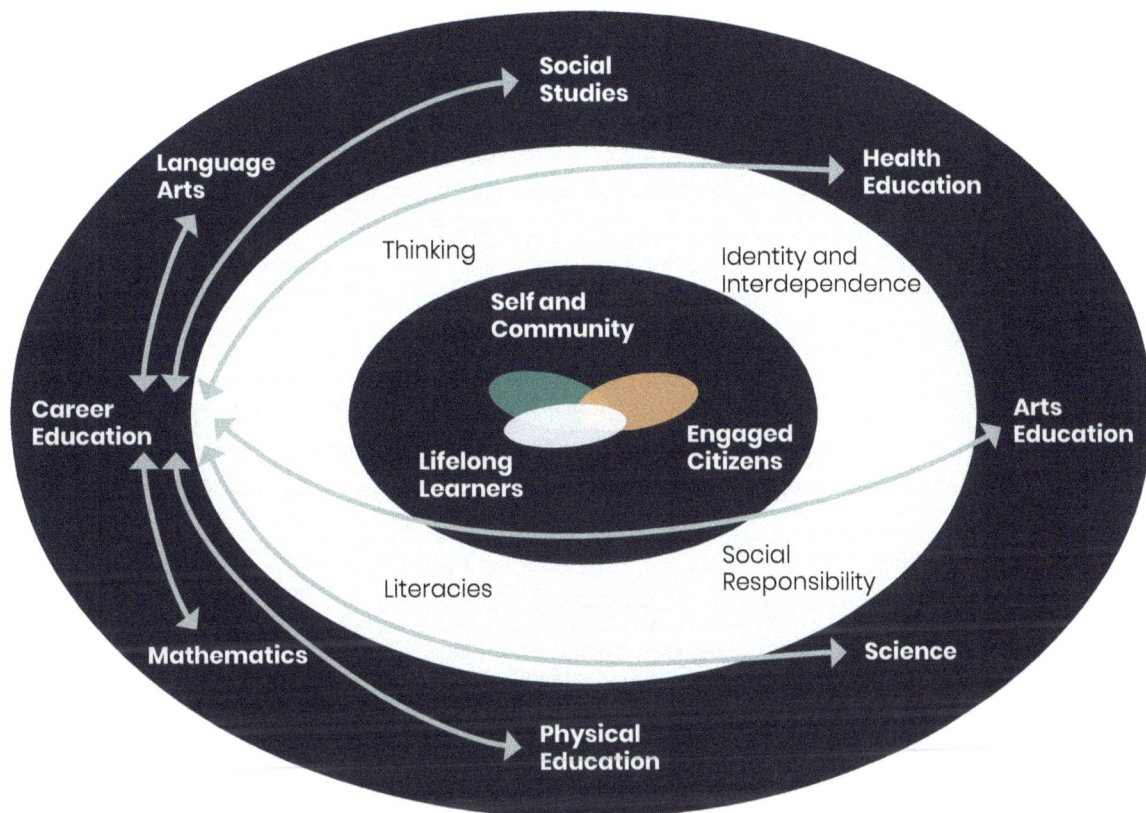

Helpful Links: Saskatchewan

The curriculum document for career education grade 6 in Saskatchewan can be found at **https://curriculum.gov.sk.ca/CurriculumFile?id=203**

A range of resources to support the implementation of the curriculum can be found at **https://curriculum.gov.sk.ca/FullResourceList?id=203**

Let's pause our journey...

Like Alberta and Saskatchewan, do you have a health and life skills type of curriculum in your own province or territory?

If so, how can this curriculum support your career-related learning?

We conclude our exploration of selected curriculum and policy documents with a focus on Québec.

Québec

In Québec, the Academic and Career Guidance Content (ACGC) is designed to "guide and equip students from Elementary 5 through Secondary V in their reflection on career planning as they prepare for their future" (Québec Ministère de l'Éducation, 2023, para. 1). The ACGC also intends to contribute to developing student motivation and perseverance. The ACGC was developed upon recommendation by members of the education community and specialists and was field tested by approximately 230 pilot schools in the public and private school systems. Over the course of a school year, students have opportunities to experience ACGC as part of subject-specific learning and other learning activities.

The ACGC continuum consists of 19 ACGC items. These items are compulsory, but they do not constitute a subject and are not evaluated. The ACGC items are organized into three areas of knowledge linked by strategies that promote student learning (see Table 14).

Table 14.
The Continuum of Academic and Career Guidance Content

Area 1: Self-knowledge

Students learn about themselves and determine their personal characteristics:
- Interests, aptitudes, values, aspirations, and strengths
- Attitudes, behaviours or perceptions that contribute to a sense of personal competency

Self-knowledge has three aspects:

Personal	*Interests and Aptitudes*	Produce a description of himself/herself in terms of interests and aptitudes
Social	*Social Influences*	Select examples where his/her attitudes, behaviour or values are influenced by others, and examples where he/she influences others
Educational	*Student Duties and Work Methods*	Compare the work methods and duties of a student with those observed in the world of work
	Strengths in the Process of Transition	Select various personal characteristics that will be useful in preparing for the transition from elementary school to secondary school

Area 2: Knowledge of the world of school

Students learn to be better prepared for the challenges that await them on their educational path:

- School transitions (from elementary to secondary school, from Secondary Cycle One to Secondary Cycle Two, from secondary school to post-secondary studies)
- Québec school system and academic choices

Area 3: Knowledge of the world of work

Students learn how to be better prepared for the challenges and requirements of the labour market:

- Making connections between the world of school, themselves, and the world of work
- Exploration of trades, occupations, and professions

How can the Québec curriculum help me?

The Québec *Making Dreams Come True* document includes a detailed section on the rationale for teaching career education in schools, and the overarching characteristics of what an effective guidance-orientated approach looks like within schools. Many of the principles outlined support the approaches we recommend in this toolkit. Of particular interest is a section with examples of what practices look like in Québec schools. This helps highlight the stages of career-related learning as an adaptable curriculum and the roles different school staff and community partners might take (Government Québec, 2002, pp. 29–32).

> **Helpful Links:**
>
> The Academic and Career Guidance Content-Learning document can be found at
> http://www.education.gouv.qc.ca/fileadmin/site_web/documents/education/adaptation-scolaire-services-comp/Continuum-COSP_01-AN.pdf
>
> A copy of *Making Dreams Come True: Achieving Success Through the Guidance-Orientated Approach* (2002) can be found at
> http://www.education.gouv.qc.ca/fileadmin/site_web/documents/education/adaptation-scolaire-services-comp/SEC_AppOrientante_19-7030A.pdf

Experiencing the journey: How does this chapter come to life in my classroom?

This short overview in this chapter of a selected range of curriculum and policy documents provides some insight into what is happening in elementary education across Canada with regards to career-related learning. This chapter may be important for a range of different contexts and invested parties (see Table 15):

Table 15.

Who benefits from knowing about curricula and policy?

Teachers	who are supporting their students with career-related learning.
Guidance counsellors	who are delivering and managing career-related knowledge, information, and services across their schools.
School leaders and administrators	who are determining the scope of career-related learning across their schools and are establishing partnerships in their communities to support strategic planning for career-related activities.
Policy makers and curriculum advisors/ writers	who are directing courses of action across the policy life cycle, and are evaluating the role of different policy actors within career-related policy in schools.
Business and industry partners	who are making decisions as to whether to form or undertake strategies to enhance and sustain partnerships that support career-related learning in their local and broader community schools.

Evaluating the journey: How do I know this is worthwhile?

As with all career-related learning activities you undertake, being able to align your practices with your local curriculum and policy requirements is essential. Building opportunities for monitoring and evaluation of all career-related learning activities is something that should be planned for and undertaken at every stage, and knowing what the requirements are of your Ministry of Education and local districts are crucial. Some things to think about include:

- Is the curriculum and policy I am accessing still valid?
- How does the curriculum and policy help me in my delivery of my career-related learning activity?
- What help is there for gaining baseline data to evaluate my activities, lessons, courses, or program in my curriculum and/or policy documents?
- What sources of support are missing? Where might I go to fill these gaps?

Journey reflections: Key takeaways from this chapter

- Across Canada, career-related learning falls broadly into three strands. Some provinces and territories, such as British Columbia, Ontario, New Brunswick, and Yukon, have embraced a kindergarten to grade 12 (K–12) approach to career education. In other areas of the country, career education begins to emerge in grades 5 and 6 (e.g., Alberta, Saskatchewan). Still other regions do not appear to have any formal career education currently in place at the elementary level (e.g., Nunavut).

In some provinces and territories, there are specific career development and career-related policy and/or curriculum documents, however in other jurisdictions career-related learning also appears in subject specific policy and curriculum documents.

Where there are formal curricula, these provide useful pointers to worthwhile career-related learning that are easily adaptable and transferable to many contexts. Subsequently, if you are located in a jurisdiction that that has more limited curriculum, it is worth examining what is happening in other parts of Canada to support your career-related learning practices.

The value of engaging learners in the early grades in a variety of opportunities to reflect, develop self-knowledge, and build capacity to effectively explore passions and options is common across most curricula in every province and territory. These goals and aims align to the career-related learning approaches of this toolkit and support our assertion that many elementary school teachers are already undertaking elements of career-related learning with their students.

Chapter 6
Career-Related Learning Within the Career Development Field

Exploring the possibilities: What is this chapter about?

As reiterated throughout this toolkit, career-related learning does not happen within a vacuum. We have explored how, within grades 4–6, students might encounter a variety of ways to undertake career-related learning in different contexts and environments and with the help and support of a wide range of people. In addition to this community-based approach, there are a range of federal, provincial, and local organizations, systems, policies and processes that impact career-related learning in elementary schools, which can also be an important resource and source of support.

Why should I be reading this chapter?

In acknowledging that undertaking career-related learning in elementary schools does not happen in an isolated context, we invite you to explore the broader context and environment. This wide stance can be useful, as when we zoom out to examine a broader perspective, we see areas of commonality, important trends and patterns, and ways of approaching career-related learning that are inspiring and easily replicated or adapted for our own situations. In short, there is a big world of potential resources out there that can support the effective career-related learning activity in any school.

In this chapter, we introduce you to some relevant organizations, associations, guidelines, frameworks, and policies. To help you understand the scope of your broader career development environment, we have highlighted a select range of pan-Canadian, provincial, curriculum, and local resources. We do not intend this chapter to be exhaustive. Rather, it serves as a starting place and introduction to what is out there to support your practice. We encourage you to also explore your local and broader environments to find further useful sources and resources that will support your career-related learning practice and activity.

Planning and packing for the journey: What do I need to be thinking about?

We begin our exploration of potential sources of support at the pan-Canadian level and start by exploring recent projects and frameworks that guide what effective career development practice looks like across Canada.

Did you know? Supporting Canadians to Navigate Learning and Work Project

At national level in Canada, there has been a set of standards and guidelines since the early 2000's that outline the work expected of many different people who hold a variety of jobs connected with career development. Such roles might include career counsellors, career development practitioners, employment services, and guidance counsellors in schools. The Canadian Standards and Guidelines for Career Development Practitioners (S&Gs) were originally launched in early 2001. The S&Gs mapped out the professional competencies and ethical framework deemed necessary to support quality career service delivery. Though it was felt that the S&Gs had served Canadian career development practitioners (CDPs) well and efforts had been made to keep them current, it was clear that a comprehensive new competency framework, code of ethics, and approach to certifying CDPs were now needed. The Supporting Canadians to Navigate Learning and Work (2018–2021) project built on the foundation of the S&Gs to accomplish this goal.

The project was funded by the Government of Canada's Sectoral Initiatives Program and was supported by over 5,000 volunteer hours from hundreds of CDPs and subject matter experts (including educators) and coordinated and managed by the Canadian Career Development Foundation. The Supporting Canadians to Navigate Learning and Work project resulted in the following bilingual assets:

- A new definition of Career Development Professional
- The Pan-Canadian Competency Framework for Career Development Professionals
- The National Competency Profile for Career Development Professionals
- The Code of Ethics for Career Development Professionals
- A piloted national certification program that includes a robust exam, a performance assessment tool, and supplementary study guide
- Three micro-credentials for educators in the K–12 system

How can this project help me?

The Pan-Canadian Competency Framework for CDPs details the skills, knowledge, and actions demonstrated by effective career development professionals, career influencers, career educators, and thought leaders. As someone who is interested in career-related learning in elementary schools, you can use the Competency Framework to consider your knowledge, skills, and abilities, and to help you plan for growth as a career-related learning educator. For those interested in policy and curriculum, the Competency Framework offers evidence-based competency standards for designing career-related policy, curriculum and professional programs, resources, tools, and training.

> *"The Pan-Canadian Competency Framework for Career Development Professionals details the skills, knowledge, and actions demonstrated by effective career development professionals, career influencers, career educators, and thought leaders."* (Canadian Career Development Foundation, 2022)

The National Competency Profile for Career Development Professionals (National Profile) is a curation of competencies from the Competency Framework that details and describes effective performance, knowledge, understanding, and abilities for ALL Career Development Professionals regardless of role/setting. The Competency Profile helps career development practitioners understand the scope of their practice and the characteristics of the competencies needed by most CDPs to effectively perform their role.

The Code of Ethics provides professional boundaries and practical directives for professional behaviour and practice for those who offer any services or learning in career development related subjects. In the Code of Ethics, you will find helpful information about professional responsibility, relationships with others, diversity, research and professional development, assessment and evaluation, using technology, and outreach and leadership.

Helpful Links: Supporting Canadians to Navigate Learning and Work Project

The CDP Competency Framework can be found at
https://ccdp-pcdc.ca/en/cdp-competency-framework

The National Profile for career development practitioners (CDPs) can be found at
https://ccdp-pcdc.ca/en/national-profile

The CDP Professional Code of Ethics can be found at **https://ccdp-pcdc.ca/en/code-of-ethics**

Further resources and tools including the micro-credentials for educators in K–12 schools can be found at **https://ccdp-pcdc.ca/en/resources-tools**

Let's pause our journey...

How can the Supporting Canadians to Navigate Learning and Work project help you in your classroom?

What elements from the National Competency Framework and the CDP professional Code of Ethics resonate most with your professional role?

Did you know? The CMEC Reference Framework for Successful Student Transitions

Informed by Truth and Reconciliation Commission of Canada (TRCC) Calls to Action, the Council of Ministers of Education, Canada (CMEC) Reference Framework for Successful Student Transitions was developed to inform, encourage, and support jurisdictions as they respond to the changing nature of student transitions. The Reference Framework includes a brief review of the context surrounding student transitions in Canada, with the central component being a series of 11 benchmarks intended to support and promote good practice in student transitions. The 11 benchmarks are:

1. Stable and student-centred career programming is provided
2. Career management skills (CMS) are activity developed (these include skills of personal management, learning and work exploration, and life/work building)
3. Career and labour-market information is accessible, and its effective use is supported
4. Policy and programing recognize, and are tailored to, the diverse and specific needs of students
5. Learning is explicitly linked to labour-market applications
6. All students participate in work-integrated learning opportunities
7. Students learn about all post-secondary education pathways
8. Youth have access to career and transition services
9. Implementation, impact, and quality assurance are underpinned by adequate training of providers
10. Career education and service provision are assessed
11. Continuous improvement is guided by evidence and return on investment

How can the Reference Framework help me?

Though we typically associate transitions with students moving from elementary school through to high school and beyond, it is important to also consider the more frequent transitions that students make between grades. Equipping students to navigate transitions is, therefore, important at all stages of their educational journey.

The 11 benchmarks can be used at pan-Canadian, provincial/territorial, and local levels by anyone interested in career-related learning as a starting point for strengthening transition policies and programs. To support this task, this Reference Framework is accompanied by two assessment and action-planning tools, as included in the resources box below.

Helpful Links: The CMEC Reference Framework for Successful Student Transitions

A copy of the CMEC Reference Framework for Successful Student Transitions in English and French can be found at https://www.cmec.ca/Publications/Lists/Publications/Attachments/372/CMEC-Reference-Framework-for-Successful-Student-Transitions-EN.pdf
https://www.cmec.ca/Publications/Lists/Publications/Attachments/372/CMEC-Reference-Framework-for-Successful-Student-Transitions-FR.pdf

The Student Transition benchmark Self-Assessment Tool in English and French can be found at http://cmec.ca/docs/Student-Transition-Benchmark-Self-Assessment-Tool-EN.pdf
https://cmec.ca/docs/Student-Transition-Benchmark-Self-Assessment-Tool-FR.pdf

The Student Transition Action Plan Template in English and French can be found at http://cmec.ca/docs/Student-Transition-Action-Plan-Template-EN.pdf
https://cmec.ca/docs/Student-Transition-Action-Plan-Template-FR.pdf

Regional Sources of Support

We further our journey of examination of potential sources of support at the regional level and start by exploring how Atlantic Canada has developed a framework to guide what effective career development practice looks like across four provinces in the Atlantic (Eastern) region of Canada.

Did You Know? Future in Focus: Atlantic Career Development Framework for Public Education (2015–2020)

The Atlantic Career Development Framework for Public Education (the Framework) was developed in partnership with the Canadian Career Development Foundation (CCDF) to strengthen career education across public and post-secondary education in the four provinces of New Brunswick, Nova Scotia, Prince Edward Island, and Labrador and Newfoundland that make up the Atlantic region in Canada. The Framework reflects a commitment by these four provinces to enhance the provision of career development and articulates common goals, while respecting the need for each province to develop initiatives that reflect both the spirit of these common goals and the unique needs, strengths, and realities of each province. The seven goals for the framework are organized into three categories: Programs, Students, and Educators (see Table 16).

Table 16.

Three categories of the seven goals of The Atlantic Career Development Framework for public education

Programs	Students	Educators
Goal 1. Support career development using a coordinated whole school approach, orga-nized by career development themes. *Goal 2:* Implement age-appropriate career development programs, services or supports.	*Goal 3:* Promote career development as an integral part of student learning. *Goal 4:* Ensure that each student graduates with a personal career plan. *Goal 5:* Provide multiple op-portunities for students to engage in community-based/experiential learning.	*Goal 6:* Provide professional learning for educators to ensure effective and engaging career development opportunities for students. *Goal 7:* Ensure access to timely, reliable, and relevant career and labour market information.

Each province was asked to commit to developing an implementation and evaluation plan that sets out how and when they intend to achieve the goals of this framework. Provinces were pointed towards the environmental scan and the analysis that were completed as part of *Career Education in Atlantic Canada: Research and Recommendations* to map their current career development programs, services, and supports against the goals articulated in this framework.

How Can This Reference Framework Help Me?

The goals of this Framework are aimed at programs, students, and educators, and as such the Framework provides an explicit and holistic landscape of how career education can straddle all areas of curriculum across grades K–12. The universal focus also allows individuals to see where their responsibilities may lie in bringing career-related learning into the classroom and the various ways this can be achieved.

Helpful Links: Future in Focus: Atlantic Career Development Framework for Public Education (2015–2020)

A copy of the Future in Focus: Atlantic Career Development Framework in English can be found at **https://www.gov.nl.ca/education/files/Future-in-Focus-Framework-English-FINAL.pd**f

A copy of the Career Education in Atlantic Canada: Research & Recommendations an underpinning research study completed by CCDF in 2015 can be accessed at **https://ccdf.ca/wp-content/uploads/2019/01/Career-Education-in-Atlantic-Canada-Research-and-Recommendations-June-2015.pdf**

Additional resources from the Council of Atlantic Ministers of Education and Training (CAMET) is available in English and French at **https://camet-camef.ca/english/home https://camet-camef.ca/french/accueil**

Did You Know? Careers Atlantic Canada

Careers Atlantic Canada is a web-based resource with designated pages for each of the four provinces that combine to form the Atlantic Canada region. The primary focus of this resource is to highlight how the Skills for Success Framework is being utilized in each of the provinces. The website also features resources for local labour market information (LMI).

> *"Learning about Skills for Success and LMI and skill development can be enhanced when there is a multidisciplinary approach to the delivery of these lessons."* (Council of Atlantic Ministers of Education and Training, 2023)

How can the Careers Atlantic Canada website help me?

The information, resources, and learning activities contained on the website can help you support your learners in understanding the relationship between Skills for Success and a successful entry into the Labour Market. Most importantly, you and your learners can discover what each of the Skills for Success are and how they benefit personal lives at home, in the community, and in all learning environments including work.

Helpful Links: Careers Atlantic Canada

You can learn more about Careers Atlantic Canada at https://careersatlanticcanada.ca/#anchor

You can learn more about the basics of LMI at **https://careersatlanticcanada.ca/the-basics-of-lmi**

Let's pause our journey...

What interests you most about the career development work in Atlantic Canada?

What takeaways are there to help you in your own practice?

Provincial Career Development Frameworks

At this stage of our journey, we examine two examples of potential sources of support at the provincial level and start by exploring how New Brunswick has developed a framework to guide what effective career development practice looks like across its province. We also consider the British Columbia's *Framework for Enhancing Student Learning*.

Did you know? New Brunswick: preK–12 Career Development Framework

In 2016, the province of New Brunswick published Ten-Year Education Plans for both the Anglophone and Francophone sectors titled *New Brunswick: Everyone at their best* (Province of New Brunswick, 2016a), and the *Francophone 10-year education plan* (Province of New Brunswick, 2016b) respectively.

The Anglophone sector of the New Brunswick Department of Education and Early Child Development (EECD) has been actively working on the advancement of career education in K–12 to achieve the outcomes in the 10-Year Education Plan. The resulting career education strategy *Career Connected Learning* and its associated best practices provide a foundational understanding of how to best prepare young people for the future. Similarly, the Francophone sector of the Department of Education and Early Childhood Development launched the *Allumer l'étincelle* campaign with the goal to educate families, community members, and various professionals about the role they can play in helping students explore career and life readiness plans—the first objective of the *Francophone 10-year education plan* (Province of New Brunswick, 2016b).

To offer more guidance and support as the EECD continue to work towards making career connected learning cross-curricular, a new *preK–12 Career Development Framework* was launched across New Brunswick in 2023. The framework aims to provide an important next step in assisting schools, educators, families, and students in understanding what competencies, knowledge, and other attributes will bring students towards their preferred future.

> *"A successful New Brunswick framework will ensure that all students are helped from an early age to think about their potential futures and how they might achieve their ambitions."* (New Brunswick Department of Education and Early Childhood Development, 2023, p. 6)

How can the preK–12 Career Development Framework help me?

The preK–12 Career Development Framework was crafted to reflect the current and developing economic environment and outline effective provision and delivery of career development work in schools based on robust and up-to-date evidence. The framework acknowledges that career development evolves throughout a student's time in school, intensifying through middle and high school as students are supported to explore options and prepare for transition out of elementary and secondary school. Subsequently, you can review valuable examples from the Framework to help you create and deliver effective, evidence-based, grade and stage of development appropriate career-related learning in your school.

Did you know? British Columbia: Framework for Enhancing Student Learning

The Framework for Enhancing Student Learning is British Columbia's approach to continuous improvement in public education and is intended to facilitate improvement of student learning outcomes and equity within those outcomes. The Framework brings a formalized approach to the planning and reporting expectations for all school districts with a focus on improving student learning and enhancing the intellectual, social, and career development of all students in the K–12 education system.

How can the Framework for Enhancing Student Learning help me?

The Framework for Enhancing Student Learning places emphasis on accountability and evidence-informed decision making to support a system-wide program of continuous improvement. Consequently, significant attention is placed on providing resources for strategic planning, data collecting, and report generating aspects of program delivery. These resources might be helpful if you are looking to build your own evidenced-based practices in your school and/or district. For example, on page 30 you can download a document that provides some guidance on how to effectively write descriptive statements for planning and evaluation purposes.

Career Development Organizations and Associations

There are a variety of career development organizations and associations across Canada that provide career development professionals the opportunity to connect with practitioners in other provinces. Some act as an advocacy voice for members and the profession, while others offer supports such as professional development opportunities and various resources. We have particularly focussed on selected organizations and associations that are connected too, or who undertake work with schools. Please note there are many other organizations, and we encourage you to seek out what is available in your province and beyond that you feel best aligns to your needs.

Did you know? Canadian Council for Career Development (CCCD)

The CCCD is a self-initiated and self-funded umbrella group for career development associations and related partner groups from across Canada. CCCD promotes a national advocacy voice for the career development profession and provides a vehicle for international outreach and engagement of the career development field.

How can CCCD help me?

The CCCD is a good resource for directing you to regional career development associations and for accessing resources should you wish to undertake specific career development focused training, professional development, and/or certification. Interestingly, the CCCD oversees the Canada Career Month celebrations held across Canada during the month of November. During this month, career development activities, programs, initiatives, and practice are celebrated. This would be an amazing opportunity for you to also celebrate the career-related learning that is happening in your classroom and or school.

> **Helpful Links: Canadian Council for Career Development**
>
> More information on who the CCCD are can be found at **http://cccda.org**
>
> More information on training and certification can be found at **http://cccda.org**

Did you know? CERIC

CERIC is a charitable organization that seeks to advance education and research in career counselling and development, to increase the economic and social well-being of people in Canada. It funds projects to develop innovative resources that build the knowledge and skills of diverse career and employment professionals. CERIC also annually hosts Cannexus, Canada's largest bilingual career development conference, and publishes the country's only peer-reviewed journal, *Canadian Journal of Career Development*

How can CERIC help me?

For many years, CERIC has funded a range of projects connected to career-related learning and career development in the K–12 system. CERIC works with Canadian and International career development researchers, educators, and practitioners to develop freely available resources that support the effective delivery of a range of career-related services and programs across Canada.

Helpful Links: CERIC

More information on who CERIC and what their strategic mandates are can be found at **https://ceric.ca**

Information on the range of projects CERIC has supported (including this one) can be found at **https://ceric.ca/projects/**

Resources to support you in undertaking career-related learning in your school can be found at **https://ceric.ca/resources/**

Information of the work of Dr. Millie Cahill and Dr. Edith Furey can be found at **https://ceric.ca/2017/10/research-finds-not-early-think-career-development-young-children/**

A resource to support newcomer youth that can easily be adapted for grades 4–6 can be found at **https://ceric.ca/publications/bridging-two-worlds-supporting-newcomer-and-refugee-youth/**

Did you know? Canadian Career Development Foundation (CCDF)

The Canadian Career Development Foundation (CCDF) are a non-profit organization that works to advance career services and the capacity of the career development profession to respond to the needs of all Canadians. The CCDF are a nationally and internationally recognized leader of career development that focuses on applied research, policy consultation, resource development, and professional capacity building.

How can CCDF help me?

The CCDF has developed numerous resources including some freely available guides in English for holding workshops with parents of children in grades 5–8. We encourage you to explore these resources and think about how you might apply them to your own contexts.

Helpful Links: Canadian Career Development Foundation

More information about who the CCDF are can be found at **https://ccdf.ca/who-we-are/**

More information on the research conducted by CCDF can be found at **https://ccdf.ca/research/**

More information on the training and resources including parents' guides provided by CCDF can be found at **https://ccdf.ca/training-resources/**

Labour Market Information (LMI)

Labour market information (LMI) is any information that assists people to make informed decisions about the labour market. The labour market is a general concept that describes the interaction between the number of people who are available for and are seeking work and the number of work opportunities that are available. LMI is available on occupations or industry, and it is used to help you make important and effective decisions about education and training, where you might obtain your first job or how to build your career. Having quality and timely LMI also allows governments, industries, organizations, and individuals to prepare for the economy of tomorrow, by ensuring the right people are available for future work and by encouraging the development of new skills which can take economies in new, productive directions.

Did you know? Labour Market Information Council (LMIC)

The Labour Market Information Council (LMIC) is a not-for-profit organization established to identify and implement pan-Canadian priorities to address the need for more consistent and accessible labour market information for Canadians.

How can LMIC help me?

In addition to providing sources of LMI, the LMIC offers a number of resources that you can use to inspire a range of career-related learning activities in your classroom. For example, *Work-Words* is an online labour market encyclopedia that provides a range of key definitions. These could be used as a prompt for a range of career-related learning activities. Google Earth can also be used to explore your local and wider area. Students can learn about the different types of work that happen in their locale, and using LMI in these types of activities provides a wide variety of opportunities for students to develop their investigative and self-directed inquiry skills.

Helpful Links: Labour Market Information Council[1]

You can find out more about the Labour Market Information Council at https://lmic-cimt.ca/about/

You can access the WorkWords at **https://lmic-cimt.ca/lmi-resources/workwords/**

You can access a range of resources about skills at **https://lmic-cimt.ca/lmi-resources/skills/**

---

1   Labour Market Information resources could be helpful for activities provided near the end of this chapter.

Key findings from our study

Resources to support teachers

The survey contained several items related to resources to support grade 4 to 6 teachers. The first items related to general teaching supports and for every one of these items, 80 to 100 percent of respondents said they had the available support (e.g., teaching resources, a supportive principal, a supportive parent group) to help them do their job. When the items asked specifically about career education, the response patterns changed. As an example, most respondents reported not having (or knowing about) a district level careers co-ordinator (or similar role) and only one respondent could identify whether curriculum documents contained information and advice about career-related learning. Sixty percent of respondents reported they were able to find career-related resources on their own and an equal number were aware of Ministry of Education resources targeted towards career learning. Of note was the high number of respondents (all respondents except one) who indicated it is difficult to complete the entire curriculum in a school year. This is important because in cases where the teacher feels pressed for time, it can be non-core subjects (e.g., career-related learning) that are cut to focus on completing academic elements of the curriculum such as literacy and numeracy.

The educator survey data provides evidence for the following findings:

- Students in grades 4 to 6 talk about jobs and careers with their teachers
- Educators focus on core teaching subjects such as literacy and numeracy and see those subjects as foundational to supporting students' future careers
- Educators see value in career-related learning and take some steps to engage in such learning
- Educators see themselves and students' families as being important in helping students think about their career path
- Educators feel positive about the supports offered to them as teachers, but less so when it comes specifically to career-related learning
- Educators embody a concept of "career" that goes beyond jobs and shows some alignment with notions of career that are articulated by career experts.

Resources to support learning at home

Parent respondents to our survey reported having resources available at home to support learning. As an example, 86% of respondents said they had access to science centres, museums, etc. near them and 96% said they had high speed internet at home, and 79% said their child's school had good internet access.

Experiencing the journey: How does this chapter come to life in my classroom?

From reading this chapter it should be clear to you that there are a wide range of frameworks, initiatives, policies, and processes to support you in delivering effective career-related learning. Such a range of possible sources of support can appear overwhelming and we suggest that if you are unfamiliar with many of these sources you begin with a select sample. As you expand your career-related learning activities, increasing the range of sources you engage with can help you with adapting and growing your practice.

Effectively delivering a range of career-related learning activities, lessons, courses, and programs requires you to draw upon your experiences as an educator, understand the roles of careers and career development, and have the skills and qualities to effectively manage relationships with colleagues, community, and industry partners. You may not have all the resources you need to support you in this endeavour, but the sources of support outlined in this chapter will provide a good start.

> *"Career development in schools is fundamentally enhanced if students have access to multiple experiential learning opportunities from K–12, including direct exposure to diverse post-secondary and work options."* (Council of Atlantic Minsters, 2015, p. 4)

Example activities for you to think about

In the next section of this toolkit, you will find a small selection of activities that we hope will inspire you to bring to life some of the topics in this chapter in your teaching practice. Please feel free to adapt these activities to suit your individual learning environment.

Activity:
What types of industries and businesses are there in our community?

Aim: To make students aware of different ways of working and local employment opportunities, highlighting STEM jobs

Activity Description:

1. Show students a photograph or map of the local area or nearest large town or city and ask them to pick out any employers without giving them clues (teacher can use the labels feature if using Google Earth, which may suggest more).
2. Working individually or in small groups, students can identify as many businesses and industries as possible.
3. To extend this activity, students can use internet searches to investigate more about particular businesses (e.g., those that occupy a large land space, those that appear to have lots of equipment parked outside and so on).
4. To further extend this activity, students can categorize businesses by size, location, type, etc.
5. Students could create a poster or presentation to share with the wider school community about what businesses and industries operate in their community.

Career Connections:

This activity can be adapted where the entire class maps the businesses on their own map of the community. Students could also compare a number of local towns and villages or compare a more densely populated area with a rural area. Students can also identify local transportation systems and local services, including schools, healthcare, and emergency service locations. Encourage students to comment on why different businesses and industries might be located in particular locations.

Activity:
Stepping Stones

Aim: To have students understand what is meant by the term "Career" and imagine a potential career pathway.

Activity Description: This activity comprises two parts. The first part is teacher-centred and involves teaching the students about what the term "career" means. The second part asks students to imagine a possible life path for themselves and how they might go about attaining that life.

Part I: What does "career" mean?

The teacher asks this question to the whole and elicits a variety of responses. Research has shown that students equate career with jobs. Jobs are an important part of a career, but we want to develop a more holistic notion of career that includes education, self-care, volunteering, recreation, social relationships, and other critical aspects of life. Once the teacher is satisfied that students understand that career can describe a life pathway and not just a job, Part II of the activity can begin.

Part II: Stepping Stones

Students will use the metaphor of "Stepping Stones" to imagine and describe a potential pathway for their life. Students are given a large piece of paper (we recommend something about 1 metre wide by 2 metres long but recognize that not all teachers have access to this size of paper. Generally, larger is better) and asked to draw stepping stones (or a similar metaphor) that represent a potential life pathway for them.

TIPS:

It can be difficult for learners at this age to imagine a life pathway. Provide some guiding questions such as, "Would you like to have a pet?" "What jobs do you think might be interesting?" "What education or preparation do you need for that job?" "Where would you like to live?" "What do you like learning about?" "What do you want to do for fun?" "How will you maintain good friendships?"

Career Connections:

The instructions should be broad so that students can take this assignment in a direction that is meaningful to them. Students at this age are just beginning to think about life goals. The purpose of this activity is not to establish a path but to spur conversation and imagination about future possibilities. Stepping stones do not need to be concrete steps. They can be something vague or aspirational such as "Figure out what jobs I like."

Activity:
Jobs of the future

Aim: To help students understand that jobs and working roles are not static. What some people do for work now, they may not be doing in the future. Jobs change and activities and tasks that people perform in jobs also changes.

Activity Description:

Take a look at the table below, which gives four reasons as to why jobs are changing. Can you match the jobs listed below to the right statement? Some jobs may appear in more than one place!

What is changing?	How can it affect jobs?	Which jobs?
New technology is being developed all the time.	New technology is an important reason that some jobs change and some jobs disappear.	
People are living longer.	People will need more healthcare, social care, and recreation.	
The skills of people around the world are improving.	There is more competition from the rest of the world in areas such as science, creative and media, and technology.	
We must take more care of the environment.	More research into saving energy and developing greener technologies.	

Games Developer
Civil Engineer
Recycling Officer
Science Teacher
Welder
Community Nurse
3D Web Designer

Motor Vehicle Technician
Care Home Assistant
Systems Analyst
Pharmacologist
Dental Hygienist
Biomedical Scientist
Electricity Generation Worker

Jobs of the future matching activity – Potential Answers

What is changing?	How can it affect jobs?	Which jobs?
New technology is being developed all the time.	New technology is an important reason that some jobs change and some jobs disappear.	• Games Developer • Civil Engineer • 3D Web Designer • Motor Vehicle Technician • Systems Analyst • Welder
People are living longer.	People will need more healthcare, social care, and recreation.	• Community Nurse • Dental Hygienist • Biomedical Scientist • Pharmacologist • Care Home Assistant
The skills of people around the world are improving.	There is more competition from the rest of the world in areas such as science, creative and media, and technology.	• Games Developer • Civil Engineer • Science Teacher • 3D Web Designer • Systems Analyst
We must take more care of the environment.	More research into saving energy and developing greener technologies.	• Civil Engineer • Recycling Officer • Motor Vehicle Technician • Electricity Generation Worker • Welder

Career Connections:

To extend this activity students can be asked to predict what jobs might exists in the future and also what qualifications, training, or skills people might need to perform these jobs. An interesting twist on this activity is to ask students what jobs they think will be done by robots in years to come.

Activity:
What is changing?

Aim: Students will understand that jobs change over time and know which industries and job roles have been affected by such change in their local and broader communities.

Activity Description:

1. Using information from what types of businesses and industries are there in our community activity, students can create a timeline showing how jobs have changed over the years. This can be a pictorial representation or written description.
2. What do they notice about the number of jobs available to people today?
3. How have the industries changed? For example, are there now more service industries?
4. What factors have affected jobs over the centuries?
5. Why might you find clusters of certain types or jobs in the city or country? For example closeness to transport links, universities, natural resources.
6. Which way might jobs go in the future?
7. Discuss as a group and include in discussion whether some of the jobs included on the timeline for today and the future are available in the local area.

Career Connections:

To extend this activity students can investigate how local differences in job opportunities mean that students may have to travel to have greater access to certain job. For example, in an area such as science, there can often be more variety in terms of opportunities in cities.

You can also explore how increases in sectors such as green (low carbon) technologies, the creative and media industries and healthcare mean that degree level qualifications are required (e.g., nursing now requires a degree).

Evaluating the journey: How do I know this is worthwhile?

As with all career-related learning activities you undertake, thinking carefully about what is working well and what is not working so well is crucial. Building opportunities for monitoring and evaluation of all career-related learning activities is something that should be planned for and undertaken at every stage, and assessing the value of your sources of support is no different. Some things to think about include:

- How relevant was the source of support to my needs?
- Is it current, reliable, and evidence-based?
- How does the source of support help me in my delivery of my career-related learning activity?
- How does the source of support help me meet my learners needs?
- Can I use the source of support to help me gain baseline data to evaluate my activities, lessons, courses, or program?
- What sources of support are missing? Where might I go to fill these gaps?

Journey Reflections: Key takeaways

Career-related learning does not occur within a vacuum. It is impacted by your context (e.g., provincial and district policies, community demographics, and the learners in the classroom).

There are a variety of organizations and associations at federal, regional, provincial and territorial, and more localized levels that support and provide resources for effective career-related learning in elementary schools.

Though we typically associate transitions with students moving between elementary school, through to high school and beyond, it is important to also consider the more frequent transitions that students make between grades. Equipping students to navigate transitions is important at all stages of their educational journey.

Sourcing and exploring resources from beyond your own immediate jurisdiction can be beneficial. The sources of support outlined in this chapter will provide you many tools to develop your library of resources. There are exciting and worthwhile practices across all of Canada!

Chapter 7
Concluding the Teaching Toolkit Journey

Reflecting on our learning

We conclude this teaching toolkit by reflecting on what we have learned and the main messages we have tried to share with you on this journey. We hope you also have your own takeaways that will inspire your ongoing journey in striving to provide effective career-related learning opportunities for your students.

Career-related learning aligns to the teaching and learning mission
We commenced this toolkit journey through exploring and understanding what career-related learning is and how much it aligns with the day-to-day teaching and learning activities typically seen in the grade 4–6 classroom. Our approach has been one of celebrating the important work that educators across Canada undertake in helping their students learn about themselves, discover their passions and interests, and develop a range of knowledge, aptitudes, and skills that will serve them well on their life journeys.

Career-related learning matters
Career and *career-related* learning must be sensitively understood and applied in the elementary school context. Children should be learning about themselves and their interests and discovering where these explorations might take them. Though we are mindful in how we approach career-related learning in elementary schools, we emphasize its immense value. Career-related learning matters! When students engage in a wide range of experiences in different contexts and environments, they see a variety of new opportunities and develop their knowledge and skills. Importantly, career-related learning recognizes that students are on a journey through their learning and life that will include work, family, friendships, recreation, and play. Each child's journey matters, is complex, and needs to be effectively supported.

Delivering effective career-related learning is an ongoing journey
As we end our toolkit journey, we hope all educators can better understand and showcase the various ways that their teaching practices introduce and develop foundational career-related skills. When teachers embed healthy habits of mind and being, social and emotional skills, self-confidence, and self-efficacy into practice, they create effective

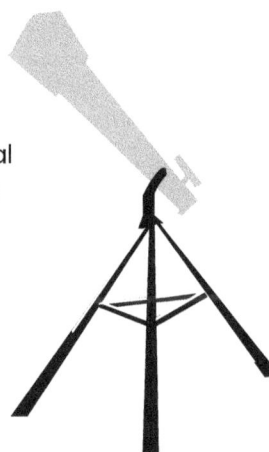

career-related learning and nurture foundational skills. We also hope that your engagement with this toolkit is indicative of your ongoing journey of delivering effective and worthwhile career-related learning.

Concluding thoughts

In this teaching toolkit, we set out to take you on a journey of exploration of career-related learning with several overarching aims. First, we have explored with you how career-related learning is understood as it relates to your teaching with students in grades 4–6. We also collated knowledge of different practices in delivering effective career-related learning to increase our understanding of the barriers and enablers (conditions and strategies) to worthwhile practices. In travelling this journey, we were able to document some innovative and creative practices and example activities including the use of digital technology to deliver career-related learning, illustrating some of the ways educators can work with their local and broader communities to support effectiveness in the delivery of career-related learning. We hope that we have offered you a comprehensive and adaptable teaching toolkit.

In our ongoing work with young students, we understand that we are always on a journey of some kind. Whether it is getting to know our incoming cohort for the new school year, adapting our practice to reflect curriculum change or renewal, teaching a new grade, or moving to a new school or place of work. Some of these journey components are slight shifts in direction, some are completely new pathways to travel. Career-related learning is a catalyst for growth and change. Like any important and meaningful journey, it can be daunting to plan but exciting to travel. As we have re-iterated throughout this toolkit, career is about focusing on life, learning, and work of individuals. The process of undertaking effective career-related learning with young people will equip them to be better prepared to navigate their lives in and out of school. We cannot over-emphasize how much this learning matters!

We hope that this teaching toolkit helps you to see that you are already undertaking many effective career-related learning practices in your every-day teaching and learning practice. What this teaching toolkit does is show you that you are not undertaking this responsibility alone and there are many educators, career development professionals, associations, organizations, policies, and curricula to support you. The activities shared in this toolkit are a great starting point and may serve as inspiration for you to develop your own activities.

As we have created this teaching toolkit, we have sought to underscore the value of undertaking career-related learning with your students. We firmly believe that focusing on providing opportunities for young people to develop skills, knowledge, and aptitudes that support their ongoing career is one of the most valuable contributions we can make through our professional lives. We agree this is an enormous responsibility and a significant challenge in many instances, but in investing in young people's futures you are empowering them to build fulfilling and meaningful lives and equipping them to make positive contributions across Canada and beyond. What could possibly be a more valuable and important journey to take?

References

Amundson, N. (2010). *Metaphor making: Your career, your life, your way.* Ergon Communications.

Andrews, D. & Hooley, T. (2023) *The career leaders handbook* (2nd ed.). Trotman Publishing.

Barnes, S-A., Bimrose, J., Brown, A., Gough, J., & White, S. (2020). *The role of parents and carers in providing career guidance and how they can better be supported.* http://wrap.warwick.ac.uk/134365/13/WRAP-role-parents-carers-providing-careers-guidance-how-they-can-be-better-supported-international-evidence-report-Barnes-2020.pdf

British Columbia Ministry of Education. (n.d.). *BC's curriculum, career education.* https://curriculum.gov.bc.ca/curriculum/career-education#

Cahill, M., & Furey, E. (2017). *The early years career development for young children: A guide for educators.* CERIC.

Cahill, M., & Furey, E. *The early years career development for young children: A guide for parents.* CERIC.

Career Development Institute. (2017). *Definitions: Career development and related roles.* https://www.thecdi.net/write/CDI_Definitions_FINAL.pdf

CERIC. (n.d.). *Guiding principles of career development.* https://ceric.ca/wp-content/uploads/2018/06/Principles-of-Career-and-Career-Development-Poster-8.5-x-11-English-1.pdf

Chavaudra, N., Moore, N., Marriott, J. & Jakhara, M. (2014). Creating an evidence base to support the development of a holistic approach to working with children and young people in Derbyshire: A local authority case study on the integration of social pedagogy in children and young people's services. *International Journal of Social Pedagogy, 3*(1), 54–61. https://doi.org/10.14324/111.444.ijsp.2014.v3.1.006

Cohen-Scali, V., Pouyau, J., & Guichard, J. (2018). Les méthodes de life design pour la construction de soi et l'orientation professionnelle des adultes émergentes. In Masdonati, Massoudi & Rossier (eds.). *Repères pour l'Orientation* (pp. 19–48). Antipodes: Lausanne.

Council of Ministers of Education Canada. (2017). *CMEC reference framework for successful transitions.* https://www.cmec.ca/Publications/Lists/Publications/Attachments/372/

CMEC-Reference-Framework-for-Successful-Student-Transitions-EN.pdf

Council of Atlantic Ministers of Education and Training (2023). *Careers Atlantic Canada: Educators.* https://careersatlanticcanada.ca/secondary-education

European Commission, Directorate-General for Education, Youth, Sport and Culture, Key competences for lifelong learning, Publications Office (2019). https://data.europa.eu/doi/10.2766/569540

Frayer, D. A. Fredrick, W. C. and Klausmeier, H. J. (1969). *A schema for testing the level of concept mastery.* University of Wisconsin.

Gallagher-Mackay, K. (2019). *Roadmaps and roadblocks: Career and life planning, guidance, and streaming in Ontario's schools.* People for Education. https://peopleforeducation.ca/report/roadmaps-and-roadblocks/

Gallup. (2019). *Creativity in learning.* https://www.gallup.com/education/267449/creativity-learning-transformative-technology-gallup-report-2019.aspx

Government of Alberta. (2013). *Ministerial order (#001/2013) student learning.* https://education.alberta.ca/media/1626588/ministerial-order-on-student-learning.pdf

Government of Alberta. (2017). *CTF Program of Studies* https://education.alberta.ca/media/3795641/ctf-program-of-studies-jan-4-2019.pdf

Government of Ontario. (2013). *Creating Pathways to Success: An Education and Career/Life Planning Program for Ontario Schools.* Queen's Printer for Ontario. https://www.edu.gov.on.ca/eng/document/policy/cps/creatingpathwayssuccess.pdf

Government of Saskatchewan. (2008). *Career Education 6.* https://curriculum.gov.sk.ca/CurriculumHome?id=203

Hartung, P. J., Porfeli, E. J., & Vondracek, F. W. (2005). Child vocational development: A review and reconsideration. *Journal of Vocational Behaviour, 66,* 385–419. https://doi.org/10.1016/j.jvb.2004.05.006

Ho, C. (2019). *Professionals in post-secondary education: Conceptions of career influencers* [Doctoral dissertation, Simon Fraser University]. Summit Research Repository. https://summit.sfu.ca/item/18827

Inkson, K., & Amundson, N. E. (2002). Career metaphors and their application in theory and counselling practice. *Journal of Employment Counseling, 39*(3), 98–108. https://doi.org/10.1002/j.2161-1920.2002.tb00841.x

Kashefpakdel, E., Rehill, J., & Hughes, D. (2018a). *What works? Career related learning in primary schools.* The Careers & Enterprise Company.

Kashefpakdel, E., Rehill, J., & Hughes, D. (2018b). *Career-related learning in primary: The role of primary teachers in preparing children for the future.* Education and Employers Research.

Kirkpatrick, D. L. (1967). Evaluation of training. In R. L. Craig & L. R. Bittel (Eds.), *Training and Development Handbook* (pp. 87–112). McGraw Hill.

Law, B. (1996). Building on what we know: Career learning theory. in A G Watts, B. Law, J. Killeen, J. M. Kidd, & R. Hawthorn (Eds.). *Rethinking careers education and guidance: Theory, policy and practice* (pp. 29–46). Routledge.

Law, B. (2008). Changing metaphors for careers-work. *The Career-learning Café*. http://www.hihohiho.com/magazine/features/cafmetaphor.pdf

Magnuson, C. S. (2000). How early is too early to begin life career planning? The importance of the elementary school years. *Journal of Career Development, 27*(2), 89–101. https://doi.org/10.1177/089484530002700203

Merchant, S., Klinger, D., & Love, A. (2018). Assessing and reporting non-cognitive skills: A cross-Canada survey. *Canadian Journal of Educational Administration and Policy*, 187, 2–17. https://journalhosting.ucalgary.ca/index.php/cjeap/article/view/43135/43931

Millard, W., Bowen-Viner, K., Baars, S., & Menzies, L. (2019). *More than a jobs worth: making career education age-appropriate*. Centre for Education and Youth.

Millington, R (2010 November 23rd). *Different types of community*. Community Strategy Insights. https://www.feverbee.com/different-types-of-communities/

McCormick, R., Amundson, N., & Poehnell, G. (2006). *Guiding circles: An Aboriginal guide to finding career paths*. Egon Publications. https://www.iworks.org

McIlveen, P., & Creed, A. (2018). La conversation, métaphore de l'approche narrative du counseling d'orientation. In Masdonati, Massoudi & Rossier (eds.) *Repères pour l'Orientation*, pp. 361–383. Antipodes: Lausanne.

Moore, N., & Hooley, T. (2012). *Talking about career: The language used by and with young people to discuss life, learning and work*. International Centre for Guidance Studies, University of Derby.

Moore, N, Neary, S., Clark, L and Blake, H (2021*). Crucial impacts on career choices: Research to understand the influences on young people's choices in primary and secondary schools: Final report*. University of Derby. https://repository.derby.ac.uk/item/94999/crucial-impacts-on-career-choices-research-to-understand-the-influences-on-young-people-s-choices-in-primary-and-secondary-schools-executive-summary

National Career Development Association. (2011). *Career Development: A policy statement of the National Career Development Association*. https://associationdatabase.com/aws/NCDA/pt/fli/4728/false

New Brunswick Department of Education and Early Childhood Development. (2023). *Career development framework in New Brunswick*. https://www2.gnb.ca/content/dam/gnb/Departments/ed/pdf/K12/career-education-framework-rational.pdf

Niles, S. G., & Harris-Bowlsbey, J. (2017). *Career development interventions*. Pearson Publications.

Organisation for Economic Co-operation and Development. (2018). *Preparing youth for an inclusive and sustainable world: The OECD PISA global competence framework.* OECD. https://www.oecd.org/education/Global-competency-for-an-inclusive-world.pdf

Organisation for Economic Co-operation and Development. (2019). *Skills matter: Additional results from the survey of adult skills.* OECD Skills Studies, OECD Publishing. https://doi.org/10.1787/1f029d8f-en

People for Education. (2016). *The geography of opportunity: What's needed for broader student success.* People for Education Annual Report on Ontario's Publicly Funded Schools 2016. People for Education. https://peopleforeducation.ca/report/annual-report-2016/

Perry, B. L., Martinez, E., Morris, E., Link, T. C., & Leukefeld, C. (2016). Misalignment of career and educational aspirations in middle school: Differences across race, ethnicity, and socioeconomic status. *Social Sciences, 5*(35). https://doi.org/10.3390/socsci5030035

Province of New Brunswick. (2016a). *10-year education plan – Everyone at their best* (Anglophone sector). Province of New Brunswick. https://www2.gnb.ca/content/dam/gnb/Departments/ed/pdf/K12/ EveryoneAtTheirBest.pdf

Province of New Brunswick. (2016b). *10-Year Education Plan – Donnons à nos enfants unelongueur d'avance (giving our children an edge)* (Francophone Sector). Province of New Brunswick. https://www2.gnb.ca/ content/dam/gnb/Departments/ed/pdf/K12/ DonnonsANosEnfantsUneLongueurDavance.pdf

Province of New Brunswick. (2023). *Allumez L'Étincelle.* Ministère de l'éducation et du développement de la petite enfance. https://allumezletincelle.ca

Québec Ministère de l'Éducation. (2023). *Academic and career guidance content (ACGC).* http://www.education.gouv.qc.ca/en/teachers/support-and-assistance/services-educatifs-complementaires/academic-and-career-guidance-content/

Québec Ministère de l'Éducation. (2002). *Making dreams come true: Achieving success through the guidance-orientated approach.* http://www.education.gouv.qc.ca/fileadmin/site_web/documents/education/adaptation-scolaire-services-comp/SEC_AppOrientante_19-7030A.pdf

Royal Bank of Canada. (2018). *Humans wanted: How Canadian youth can thrive in the age of disruption.* RBC. https://www.rbc.com/dms/enterprise/futurelaunch/_assets-custom/pdf/RBC-Future-Skills-Report-FINAL-Singles.pdf

Royal Bank of Canada. (2019). Bridging the gap: *What Canadians told us about the skills revolution.* https://www.rbc.com/dms/enterprise/futurelaunch/_assets-custom/pdf/RBC-19-002-SolutionsWanted-04172019-Digital.pdf?_gl=1*1obnubv*_ga*MTUxMTc5MzMyMC4xNjg4MzUzMTk0*_ga_89NPCTDXQR*MTY4ODM1MzE5NS4xLjEuMTY4ODM1MzI4My41Mi4wLjA.&_ga=2.122941826.889370342.1688353194-1511793320.1688353194

Schleicher, A. (2018). Notes from our partners. In Chambers, N., Rehill, J., Kashefpakdel, E., & Percy, C. (2018). *Exploring the career aspirations of primary school children from around the world: Drawing the future*. Education & Employers. https://www.educationandemployers.org/wp-content/uploads/2018/01/DrawingTheFuture.pdf

Sellers, N., Satcher, J., & Comas, R. (1999). Children's occupational aspirations: Comparisons bygender, gender role identity, and socioeconomic status. *Professional School Counseling, 2*(4), 314–317. https://www.jstor.org/stable/42731996

Singapore Ministry of Education (2023). 21st Century Competencies. https://www.moe.gov.sg/education-in-sg/21st-century-competencies.

Stuart, R. (2014*). Learning to work: Research report*. Chartered Institute of Personnel and Development (CIPD). https://www.cipd.org/

Super, D. (1980). A life-span, life-space approach to career development. *Journal of Vocational Behaviour, 16*(3), 282–298. https://doi.org/10.1016/0001-8791(80)90056-1

Thomsen, R. (2012). Guidance in communities - A way forward? *Journal of the National Institute for Career Education and Counselling, 28*, 39–45. https://doi.org/10.20856/jnicec.2806

Thomsen, R. (2017). *Career guidance in communities: A model for reflexive practice*. University of Derby. https://repository.derby.ac.uk/download/4a755b501248a7ef783913c4c0cdffe8c86d7b62ec2cb9a79015cb87b27bd2fd/793369/Career%20guidance%20in%20communities%20final_02052017%20.pdf

Watts, A. G. (2004). Career guidance and public policy: Bridging the gap. OECD Publishing.

Watson, M., & McMahon, M. (2005). Children's career development. A research review from a learning perspective. *Journal of Vocational Behaviour, 67*(2), 119–132. https://doi.org/10.1016/j.jvb.2004.08.011

Watson, M., & McMahon, M. (2008). Children's career development: Metaphorical images of theory research & practice. *Career Development Quarterly, 57*(1), 75–83. https://doi.org/10.1002/j.2161-0045.2008.tb00167.x

Wilson, J., & Jackson, H. (1998). *What are adults' expectations and requirements of guidance? A millennium agenda?* The Guidance Council.

Appendix A:
Skills Cards (for Matching Game)

Writing

Being honest with myself

Math

Creativity and Innovation

Collaboration or Teamwork

Being responsible

Asking good questions

Being organized

Setting goals

Reading

Communicating ideas
to others

Having empathy for
others

Using computers

Recognizing my own
moods

Being adaptable or
flexible

Staying healthy

Problem solving

Listening to others

Confidently speaking
to others

Appendix B:
Experience Cards (for Matching Game)

Traveling outside of Canada	Babysitting
Working as a cashier	Using social media safely
Being a parent	Designing a house
Organizing a fundraiser	Starting a garden
Coaching sports	Being a scientist

Working at an animal shelter

Flying an airplane

Being a YouTuber

Building a bridge

Resolving a fight between friends

Creating an ad campaign

Putting on a talent show

Teaching

Camping

Cooking a meal

Appendix C:
Fundamental Skills
(for Show-Off Your Skills)

Adaptability	Innovation
Collaboration	Healthy Habits
Creativity	Physical Fitness
Communication	Reading

Patience	Writing
Self-Discipline	Problem-Solving
Computer Skills	Empathy
Math	Responsibility

Appendix D:
Research Study Numbers
of Participants (n)

Participant Type	English	French
Educators	85	2
Parents	108	1
Students	71	4
Business/Industry	13	0
Pre-Service Teachers	35	0

Praise for Exploring Possibilities! Journeying Through Career-Related Learning in Grades 4–6

"This career development in children toolkit Exploring Possibilities! Journeying Through Career-Related Learning in Grades 4-6, is a comprehensive career development resource for elementary teachers. The toolkit offers detailed research to build a powerful rationale for using a career development lens in elementary school work and activities and reshapes the word 'career' into a thoughtful and imaginative journey full of learning and experiences that ignites students' life journeys."
Adriano Magnifico, Career & Entrepreneurship Consultant, Louis Riel School Division, Manitoba, Canada.

"The Exploring Possibilities! Journeying Through Career-Related Learning in Grades 4–6: A Teaching Toolkit is an important project in education but more specifically, in the area of elementary career education. The resulting teaching toolkit is a resource that can not only inform the practice of educators but to support a shift in mindset leading to the significant and intentional delivery of career development for elementary learners. The use of the toolkit will without a doubt have a lasting impact on the lives of our learners. It is with great hope that we will see its use across the relevant grades in allowing for more universally accessed career connected learning."
Tricia Berry, Learning Specialist, Educational Support Services, Education and Early Childhood Development, Government of New Brunswick, Canada.

"As both a Grade 4 teacher and a Career Coach, I have been searching for quality career-related learning materials for my students. The Exploring Possibilities! Journeying Through Career-Related Learning in Grades 4–6: A Teaching Toolkit was the resource I was looking for. It seamlessly blends current research with practical, classroom-ready activities. This manual for career education will prove invaluable to both experienced career educators and those new to the topic. The teaching toolkit makes it easy to bring career-related learning to our elementary students in meaningful, age-appropriate ways."
Michele Murphy, Elementary Teacher and Certified Career Development Practitioner, Toronto, Ontario.

"As research is increasingly pointing to the critical role of career development at earlier ages, this Toolkit is such a timely resource. It offers a powerful blend of conceptual clarity, linkages to research, tailored strategies, and practical tools/activities for classroom or community application. Any educator or career influencer working with children will want this Toolkit as their go-to guide."
Sareena Hopkins, Executive Director, Canadian Career Development Foundation, Ottawa, Canada.

"This is a timely and important new book. The Exploring Possibilities! Journeying Through Career-Related Learning in Grades 4–6: A Teaching Toolkit represents an important step forward in addressing a severely neglected subject. It responds to a growing recognition that truly effective career development will begin well before secondary education. Elementary (primary) schools have important roles to play in helping children to understand the links between their education and future possible selves and to question deep-seated assumptions about the careers that are reasonable for them to pursue. In these ways, early career development nurtures the spirit of curiosity and exploration that optimises successful engagement through education and transitions into fulfilling employment."
Dr. Anthony Mann, Senior Policy Analyst (Career Readiness), Organisation for Economic Cooperation and Development.

"This toolkit offers an interesting perspective on career-related learning throughout Canada. Its innovative and creative activities can serve as inspiration for educators who wish to initiate and develop career-related skills within their community. The use of this toolkit can benefit students, helping them develop various facets of their lives, including healthy habits, social and emotional skills, self-confidence, and more, as they prepare to embrace their future."
Dr. Vicky Prévost, Professeure adjointe, Sciences éducation - École de counseling et d'orientation, Université Laval, Quebec, Canada.

"This teaching toolkit offers valuable insights into the integration of career-related learning within elementary education. While its primary focus is on preparing young students for future opportunities, it subtly emphasizes the importance of cultivating foundational skills such as healthy habits, social and emotional competence, self-confidence, empathy, and collaboration. These skills not only support career development but also contribute to character development and lifelong flourishing. By recognizing that elementary education plays a vital role in helping children discover their passions and aspirations, this toolkit aligns with our commitment to holistic individual development. It provides educators with a valuable resource to foster both career readiness and the long-term well-being of young minds."
Professor Tom Harrison, Director of the Jubilee Centre for Character and Virtues, Deputy Pro-Vice Chancellor for Education Innovation, University of Birmingham, UK.

"Career-learning activities are important for all students; they are engaging and often foster motivation to do other activities in school. However, the students who gain the most from the activities are children from low-skilled and low-economic backgrounds which makes this toolkit an important contribution. This Exploring Possibilities! Journeying Through Career-Related Learning in Grades 4-6 A Teaching Toolkit inspires practitioners as well as policymakers and researchers to share that career is 'A lifelong journey of learning about oneself and the individual interactions you have with learning, work, and life experiences.' And that a career is about the life you want to lead – not just a job, occupation or profession. It involves deciding among possible and preferred futures. It answers: 'Who do I want to be in the world?' 'What kind of lifestyle am I seeking?' and 'How can I make an impact?' The toolkit helps readers to see that their understanding of career brings norms and expectations regarding work and life into the classroom. This toolkit supports teachers, educators and parents to be reflective about this and investigate their own norms and assumptions."
Dr. Rie Thomsen, Professor of Career Guidance, Aarhus University, Denmark.

"As an elementary school teacher, I know the importance of developing foundational skills in children. This is a hugely important part of my practice. This toolkit gives specific, practical teaching (and assessment!) strategies for developing skills such as collaboration, responsibility, and self-regulation. While there is a "career" focus to the toolkit, the truth is that these skills are useful in school, at home, and everywhere in life."
Paola Sallusti - Elementary teacher, British Columbia, Canada.

www.ingramcontent.com/pod-product-compliance
Lightning Source LLC
Chambersburg PA
CBHW052342210326
41597CB00037B/6229